Chaos Engineering for AI Infrastructure

Fault injection and resilience testing for GPUs, model serving, RAG pipelines, and agentic systems on Kubernetes

Neel Trove

Published by: GitforGits

www.gitforgits.com

Printed in India

First Printing: August 2026

ISBN: 978-93-49174-77-1

Cover Design by: Kitten Publishing

Prologue

Truth be told, I've taken out a fair few servers on purpose.

Back in 2016, I first got my hands on a virtual machine behind a payments API, using a shell script and way more confidence than the situation warranted. Since then, I've tried pretty much every fault injection tool out there. I remember when Chaos Monkey was all about terminating instances and hoping for the best. Then Gremlin made Chaos a product you could buy. The community decided that experiments should be declarative, so Chaos Toolkit was the obvious choice. When Kubernetes took over and the custom resource became the unit of work, Litmus and Chaos Mesh happened. Then there are ChaosBlade, Pumba, Powerfulseal, ChaosD, and a bunch of internal tools that most people won't have heard of.

They all taught me the same lesson, and I took it to mean the whole lesson, but I was wrong. If you break something, you can check the graph to see if the architecture is sound. The loop is fast, the feedback is unambiguous, and the satisfaction is real. An engineer can run a pod delete before lunch and find out something true about their system by the time they sit down.

Then I started working on systems with a language model in the request path, and my instruments went quiet. When it first happened, I thought I'd probably messed something up. We had really messed up the retrieval service, and every dashboard said everything was fine. Latency held. The error rate was zero. Every replica was ready. The experiment looked absorbed, which is the verdict I would have written down and filed. Two weeks later, one of the support leads mentioned that the drafts had been getting worse since the day of our experiment, and that her team had started doing manual lookups again without telling anyone.

Nothing in my toolchain had lied to me. Every tool measured exactly what it was built to measure, which is whether infrastructure survived. Not one of them checked if the system was still working well. That's what this book is all about. It's not a gap in the tooling, and getting a better fault injector won't fix it. The gap comes down to what we decide to measure and when we choose to measure it. For most teams, that was long before anyone put a probabilistic component into production. Our envelopes, alerts and postmortem templates were all designed to cover all the bases.

I've spent the last ten years learning how to break things loudly. This book looks at the less obvious side of the problem. In the next few chapters, we're going to run 41 experiments on one application. About half of them will give you a result that the system doesn't report. It's not a dig at anyone's engineering, since the systems in question are competently built and mostly behave well.

This book is all about testing and closing the gap between infrastructure health and output quality, and how easily that gap can be filled for weeks by a failure that's gone unnoticed.

Content

Preface

How long do you think it would take you to notice if your AI system started giving worse answers? Honestly, for most teams, it's weeks, and the news comes from a customer. Chaos engineering answers that question for infrastructure in about thirty seconds, because if a server goes down, it either reroutes or it doesn't. And language models completely shatter all those assumptions. Their output varies for real, their decay builds up instead of happening straight away, and those failures are confident, plausible, and wrong while latency, error rate, and pod health stay exactly where they should be.

This book sets out the new framework for AI infrastructure. You'll find that, working through one support-assistant application across twelve chapters, everything moves from defining steady state for probabilistic systems to injecting faults at every layer, including accelerators, inference servers, model artefacts, retrieval pipelines, model APIs, autonomous agents, distributed training and the monitoring stack itself.

Just to be clear, the toolchain is intentionally kept small. The LitmusChaos orchestrates, the Chaos Mesh reaches the kernel and filesystem, and the mitmproxy handles the content-level faults that neither can touch, extended with custom injectors where nothing suitable exists. So, every experiment comes to one of these four conclusions, and then the last chapter sums them all up as a programme scorecard.

In this book you will learn to:

- Write down what "working correctly" means when your system's output legitimately varies.
- Break GPUs and inference servers on purpose, with a restore path that always runs.
- Spot the failures that keep every dashboard green and every alert silent.
- Check model weights for damage before loading them, not after serving starts.
- Catch the model release that scores better overall while getting worse where it matters.
- Find out whether your RAG pipeline is helping, or quietly making answers worse.
- Corrupt what the model returns, then watch whether your agent notices.
- Stop your remediation agent from making an incident worse than it was.
- Prove your training checkpoints actually resume the run they claim to continue.
- Catch slow decay in hours instead of days by changing how you alert.

GitforGits

Prerequisites

Whether you're a site reliability engineer, a platform engineer or a machine learning infrastructure engineer running production AI systems, if you think your monitoring can't see what really matters, you need to read this.

Codes Usage

Are you in need of some helpful code examples to assist you in your programming and documentation? Your search ends here! Our book offers a wealth of supplemental material, including code examples and exercises.

Not only is this book here to aid you in getting your job done, but you have our permission to use the example code in your programs and documentation. However, please note that if you are reproducing a significant portion of the code, we do require you to contact us for permission.

But don't worry, using several chunks of code from this book in your program or answering a question by citing our book and quoting example code does not require permission. But if you do choose to give credit, an attribution typically includes the title, author, publisher, and ISBN. For example, "Chaos Engineering for AI Infrastructure by Neel Trove".

If you are unsure whether your intended use of the code examples falls under fair use or the permissions outlined above, please do not hesitate to reach out to us at support@gitforgits.com.

We are happy to assist and clarify any concerns.

Acknowledgement

I owe a tremendous debt of gratitude to GitforGits, for their unflagging enthusiasm and wise counsel throughout the entire process of writing this book. Their knowledge and careful editing helped make sure the piece was useful for people of all reading levels and comprehension skills. In addition, I'd like to thank everyone involved in the publishing process for their efforts in making this book a reality. Their efforts, from copyediting to advertising, made the project what it is today.

Finally, I'd like to express my gratitude to everyone who has shown me unconditional love and encouragement throughout my life. Their support was crucial to the completion of this book. I appreciate your help with this endeavour and your continued interest in my career.

CHAPTER 1
WHY AI SYSTEMS FAIL DIFFERENTLY?

Any chaos engineering practice, whether it's new or old, is based on one assumption about failure. The idea is that something breaks quickly and visibly, like a server dying and a graph turning red. It did a great job of supporting infrastructure teams for about ten years. But once we add a language model to the request path, the older model just stops working. The thing is, our systems start to go wrong without throwing up any warning signs, and at the same time the quality of what we're delivering is getting worse and worse.

Across this opening chapter, we will work through why that transfer breaks and what replaces it. We will spend time with HelpMate, the support assistant we break repeatedly for the rest of the book. Our next move organises its architecture into seven layers, so every later chapter has a fixed address. Along the way, we separate evaluation work from chaos work, fix the four-word vocabulary that ends every experiment, and start our working repository on disk. By the close, we will hold a coverage map of our own blind spots.

What Limits Binary Model?

Assumption Behind Every Chaos Experiment

Well, when a team terminates a server instance in production, success carries an unambiguous shape. The instance disappears, traffic reroutes, and error rates either climb or stay flat. Within thirty seconds we know whether the architecture survived. No part of that loop requires interpretation, and no committee needs to agree on what the result meant. Such clarity is precisely why the practice spread from Netflix across the industry so quickly. An experiment whose outcome fits on a single graph is easy for anyone to defend. And, this is where our problem begins, when we carry that same loop into a stack that serves model output. We terminate a pod behind an inference service and watch the replacement come up healthy. Every infrastructure signal returns to baseline within a minute, so we record the experiment as a pass. What we never measured was whether the requests served during that minute produced sensible output. Our dashboard cannot tell us, because no metric we collect describes the shape of what the model returned.

Let us look at, how differently the two worlds report trouble. A failed disk write throws an exception that lands in a log aggregator within milliseconds. Meanwhile, a model that summarises three documents instead of five throws nothing at all, since both behaviours sit inside its normal operating range. Our monitoring stack was designed around the first case and has no vocabulary for the second. Every tool we install, every alert we write, and every runbook we maintain inherits that design. No part of the stack is broken, though it measures the wrong thing entirely.

Four Properties That Break Transfer

Our stack differs from the one Chaos Monkey was built against in four specific properties. The first concerns output, which arrives as a distribution rather than a value. A model may phrase the same correct response five different ways, and all five belong inside the acceptable range. The second property follows from the first. Our baseline is fuzzy by construction, so we cannot express health as a single threshold without discarding legitimate variation. Together these two properties defeat any pass or fail check written against exact matching, and they explain why most teams abandon the attempt early. Our third property concerns time instead, and it works on a scale no dashboard is drawn for. An infrastructure fault announces itself in seconds, whereas model degradation compounds across weeks before anyone notices. A vector index goes stale one document at a time. The fourth property is the one that should worry us most, because it inverts our instincts about severity. Our system fails by producing a confidently wrong response that looks structurally identical to a correct one. No parser rejects it, no schema validator flags it, and no latency graph moves. Only a human who knows the correct response, or a held out set that encodes it, can catch the difference.

When taken together, the four properties explain a pattern visible across the industry. Even teams with mature chaos programmes stop at the boundary of their model serving stack. They are not careless, and they are not unaware of the risk. Their mental model simply does not extend past the point where failure stops being binary. Once we accept that the measurement problem comes first, the tooling problem becomes tractable. We spend the whole of the following chapter on measurement, precisely because everything after it depends on getting that part right.

Exploring 'HelpMate' System We Try Breaking

What HelpMate Does and Who Depends On It?

We need a concrete system to break, so let us adopt one now and keep it throughout. Our application is called HelpMate, and it runs inside a mid sized payments company serving roughly twelve hundred business customers. A support organisation of one hundred and twenty agents handles about nine thousand tickets each week. They field questions about failed settlements, webhook retries, refund windows, and API error codes. Before HelpMate existed, an agent would search three separate systems by hand and assemble a reply from fragments. Their average handling time sat near eleven minutes per ticket.

Today the workflow looks different, and the difference matters for how we measure quality. An agent pastes the customer question into a console, and HelpMate returns a drafted reply within roughly two seconds. The agent then reads that draft, edits whatever seems wrong, and sends it. Sometimes the draft goes out untouched, and sometimes the agent rewrites it completely. That editing step hands us something rare, namely a continuous human verdict on output quality, produced free of charge by people who already know the correct response. We call the fraction of drafts requiring substantive edits our override rate. The same workflow yields two more signals naturally. Our escalation rate tracks how often an agent abandons the draft and routes the ticket to an engineer. The refusal rate tracks how often HelpMate declines to draft anything, because retrieval returned nothing usable. Both numbers behave in ways that reward attention. A refusal rate near zero looks healthy on first inspection, though it usually means the model invents content rather than admitting ignorance. We therefore treat refusals as a two-sided signal, where too few worry us as much as too many.

Path Single Question Travels

It helps to follow one question through the whole system, since the path determines where we can inject faults later. An agent submits the query, which arrives first at **`helpmate-gateway`**, a small Go service handling authentication, per team rate limits, and the server sent event stream that carries tokens back. The gateway forwards the request to **`helpmate-agent`**, a Python orchestrator that decides what the query needs. Some questions need nothing beyond product documentation, while others need a live account lookup or the status of an ongoing incident.

Whenever context is required, the orchestrator calls **`helpmate-retriever`**. That service embeds the query, runs a hybrid search across Qdrant, and reranks the top fifty candidates down to five. All five chunks travel back with their source identifiers attached, which lets the final reply cite where each claim originated. The orchestrator then assembles a prompt from the question, the retrieved chunks, and any tool results, before it posts everything to **`helpmate-inference`**. Our inference service runs an eight billion parameter instruct model under vLLM, with continuous batching enabled and a paged key value cache.

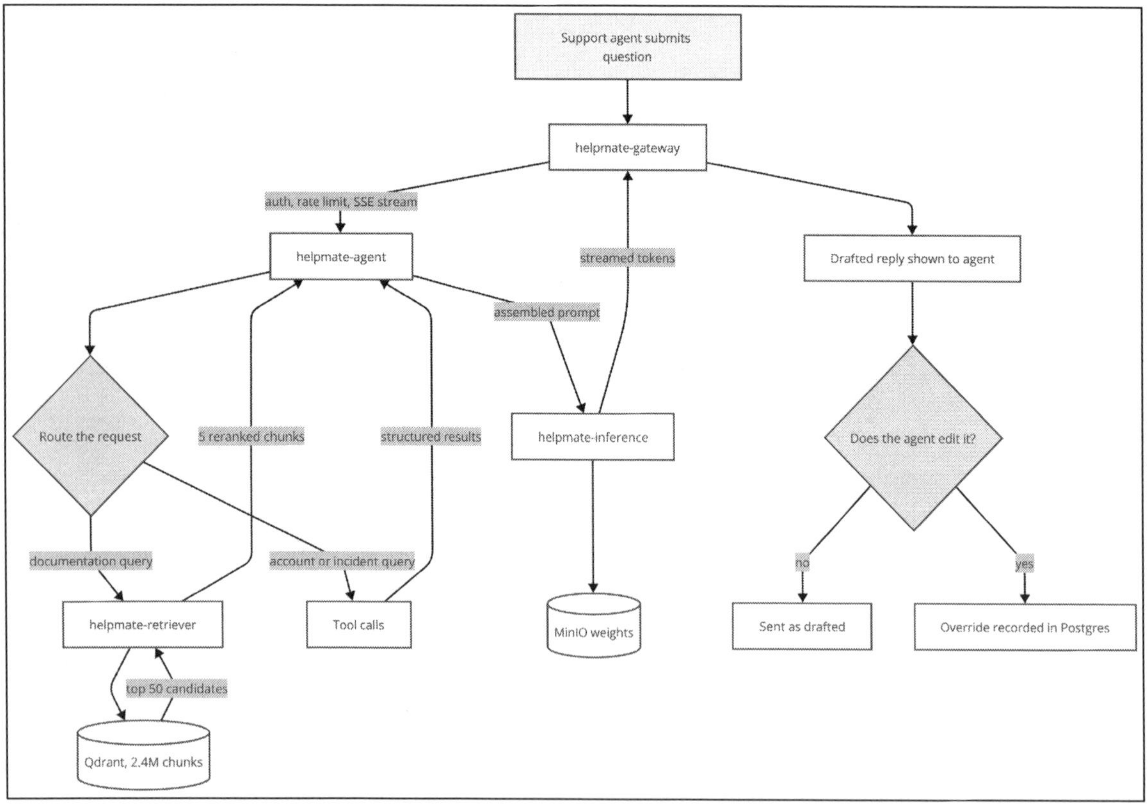

Every hop in that path can fail in at least two distinct ways. A hop can fail loudly, where it returns an error and the caller knows immediately. Alternatively, a hop can fail quietly, where it returns something well formed and wrong. Our retriever returning five irrelevant chunks looks identical to our retriever returning five perfect ones, from the perspective of every service downstream. That symmetry is the whole difficulty of the discipline in one sentence. We will spend the rest of the book learning to tell those two cases apart under controlled conditions.

Where HelpMate Keeps Its State?

Behind those services sit four stateful dependencies, and each one introduces a different failure class. Our Qdrant instance holds two point four million document chunks, drawn from product documentation, resolved tickets, and release notes. A nightly ingest job refreshes anything that changed during the previous day. The MinIO bucket stores model weights and training checkpoints, which our inference pods pull on every cold start. An OCI registry tracks model artifact versions, and Postgres records ticket metadata alongside every override an agent makes. That last table becomes our quality ground truth, so we protect it more carefully than anything else.

Our traffic through the system stays modest, which suits these purposes well. At peak, load reaches about forty requests per minute during European mornings, and median time to first token sits near three hundred and ten milliseconds. The ninety ninth percentile runs closer to nine hundred. None of this requires a large cluster or an expensive accelerator fleet, so the lab we build in Chapter 2 reproduces the whole shape at a fraction of the size. A small scale suits chaos work anyway, since a small system makes the propagation path far easier to observe.

Failure with No Infrastructure Symptom

Six Weeks of Silent Decay

The silent case deserves something concrete, since abstraction has carried us far enough. On a Tuesday in March, the nightly ingest job fails after a credential rotation nobody remembered to propagate. The job exits non zero, though its alert routes to a channel that was archived during a team reorganisation. Our service keeps running without interruption. The measured latency holds at six hundred and forty milliseconds, error rate sits at zero, and every pod reports ready throughout. Not one signal on any dashboard moves during the entire period that follows.

Meanwhile the index ages. With each passing week, the proportion of queries retrieving genuinely relevant chunks declines, because product documentation moved on and the embeddings did not. Our agents notice long before any system does. They begin adding manual lookups back into their workflow, first for the newest features and later for anything touching settlement timing. The override rate climbs from four percent to six, then to nine, and finally to eleven. Nobody plots that number against the index timestamp, since no dashboard places the two anywhere near each other.

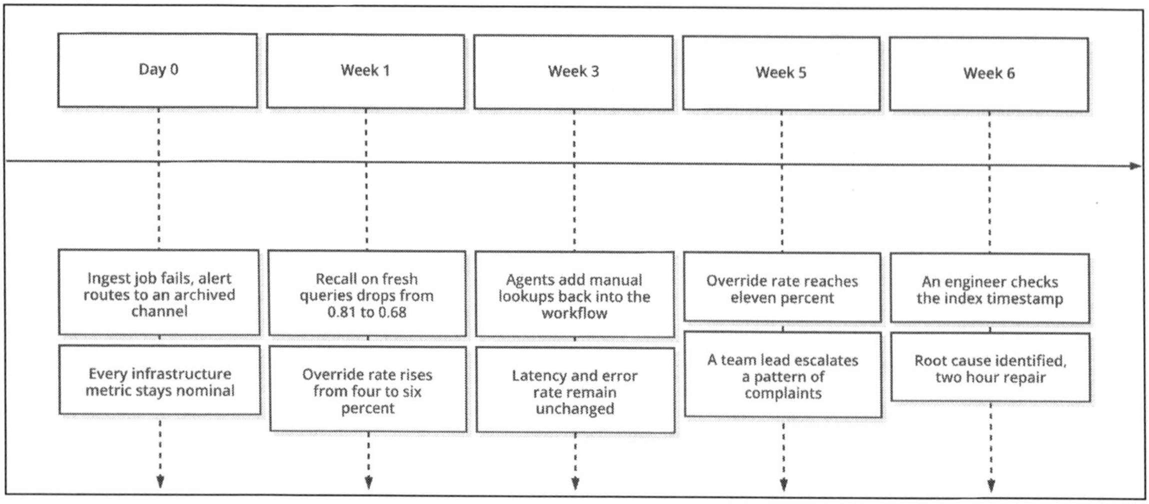

That escalation lands only after six weeks have passed. An engineer checks the index timestamp within ten minutes of picking up the ticket, and the root cause becomes obvious immediately. Our incident review afterwards records a two-hour repair alongside a six-week detection gap. Everyone reading that review will focus on the credential rotation, because credential rotations are concrete and fixable. Far fewer will focus on the detection gap, even though the gap did all the actual damage. Our chaos work exists to close gaps of exactly that kind.

Three Failures, Only One Technical

That scenario contains three separate failures, and only one of them was technical. The ingest job failed, which a simple job success alert would have caught. Behind it, retrieval quality decayed, and no signal existed anywhere to report the decay. Finally, the operations team absorbed that decay by working harder, which hid the problem from everyone upstream of them. Most incident reviews stop after the first item, because the first item has a clean owner and a clean fix. The second and third have neither, so they survive into the next quarter untouched.

This practice addresses the middle failure directly and deliberately. We inject the stale index ourselves, on a schedule we control, inside a window where somebody is watching. Our question is never whether the system survives, since we already know it survives. The real question is, whether anything in the stack moves before a human compensate? Should nothing move, we have found a blind spot worth a week of engineering effort. If instead something moves, we now know how far quality drifts before the alert finally fires.

Failure Taxonomy for AI Stack

Seven Layers Worth Breaking

We organise everything that follows around seven layers, and each layer owns a chapter later in the book:

1. At the bottom sit the accelerators, where power throttling and device loss originate.
2. Above them runs the serving layer, home to cache exhaustion and queue collapse.
3. The third layer holds model artifacts, which include registries, weights, and version changes.
4. Then comes retrieval at the fourth position.
5. The model boundary at the fifth.
6. At the sixth we place our agents and the tools they call.
7. And, our training pipelines stand slightly apart at the seventh.

The layering matters for a practical reason rather than a taxonomic one. A fault injected at any layer can surface as a symptom at a completely different layer, and our instinct sends us hunting in the wrong place. Consider a throttled GPU at layer one. The symptom our agents report is slow, truncated output, which looks like a model boundary problem at layer five. Without a map connecting the two, we spend a day debugging prompts while the real cause sits in a power limit. Every finding table in this book therefore records both the injection layer and the observation layer.

Faults That Cross Layer Boundaries

This cross-layer propagation deserves its own treatment, because it produces our most expensive incidents. We can picture the movement as flow rather than as a tree. A single fault enters at one layer and splits into several downstream symptoms, some of which trigger alerts and some of which reach users untouched. The proportion reaching users without any alert represents our blind spot. Our whole practice exists to shrink that proportion, one experiment at a time. A sankey view makes the split obvious in a way that a dependency graph never manages.

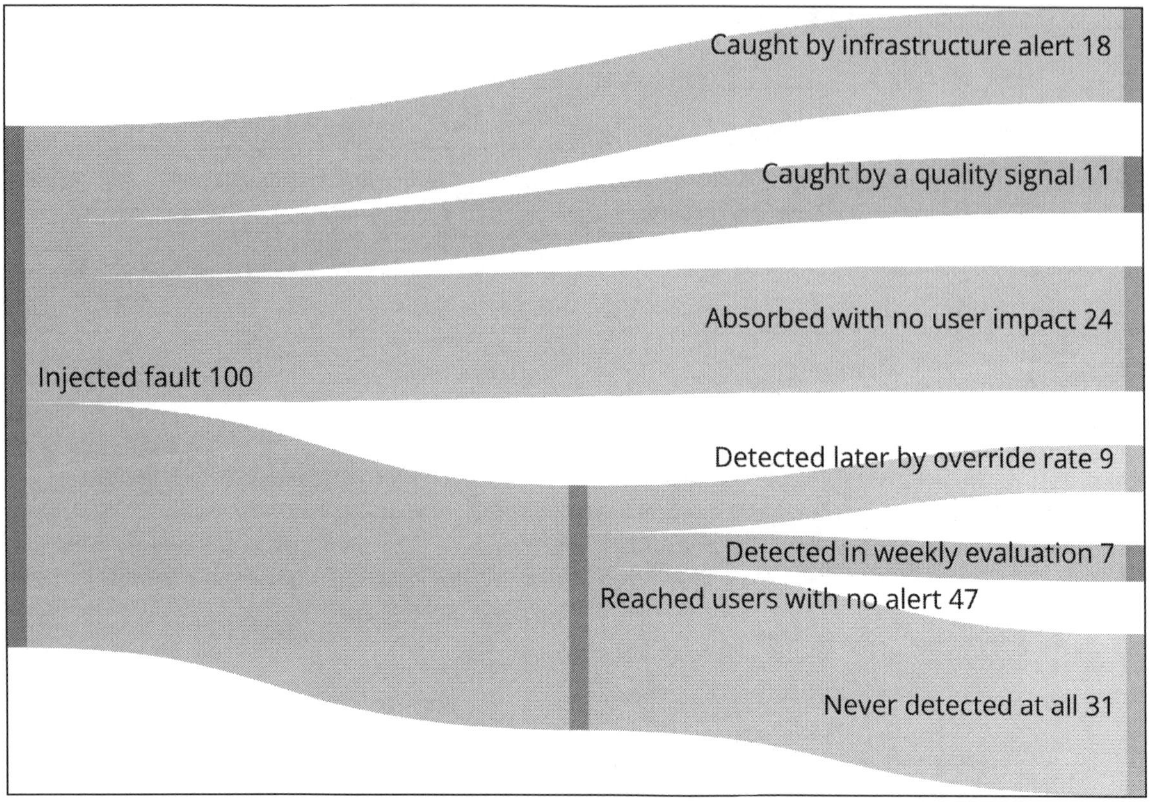

The widest band carries faults straight through to users with no alert attached. Such a picture rarely appears in postmortem documents, since postmortems only cover incidents, somebody noticed. Our chaos experiments generate the missing data, because we inject faults we already understand and then record how many stayed invisible. After a dozen experiments, we can draw this view from real numbers instead of intuition. That single artefact tends to change how leadership funds reliability work, more than any argument we could make in prose.

Why Chaos Testing Instead Monitoring?

Evaluation Suites against Production Conditions

Many teams push back at this point with a reasonable objection. They already run evaluation suites, and those suites pass. Our reply separates two different questions that sound alike. An evaluation suite asks whether the system works on inputs we designed it for. Our chaos work asks whether the system degrades gracefully once those design conditions stop holding. The first question belongs before deployment, and we resolve it once per release. Meanwhile, the second belongs in production, and we resolve it continuously, because conditions keep changing after we ship.

A worked comparison helps here. Suppose our evaluation set contains four hundred support questions with known good responses, and HelpMate scores 0.94 on it. That number tells us the system is fit to ship. Now suppose the vector index drifts by three weeks and the same set runs again. Should the score hold at 0.94, our retrieval layer has genuine redundancy. If instead it drops to 0.71 while every infrastructure metric stays flat, we have located a silent failure that no release gate would ever have caught.

Verdict Vocabulary

Every experiment in this book ends with one word, drawn from a closed set of four. We record a result as absorbed when our steady state holds inside its envelope and users notice nothing. The verdict becomes degraded once the envelope breaks and the system says so through an error, a refusal, or an alert. Our third word, cascaded, applies when the breach travels past the component we injected. Finally, silent covers the case where infrastructure stays healthy, a quality signal breaks, and nothing anywhere raises a flag.

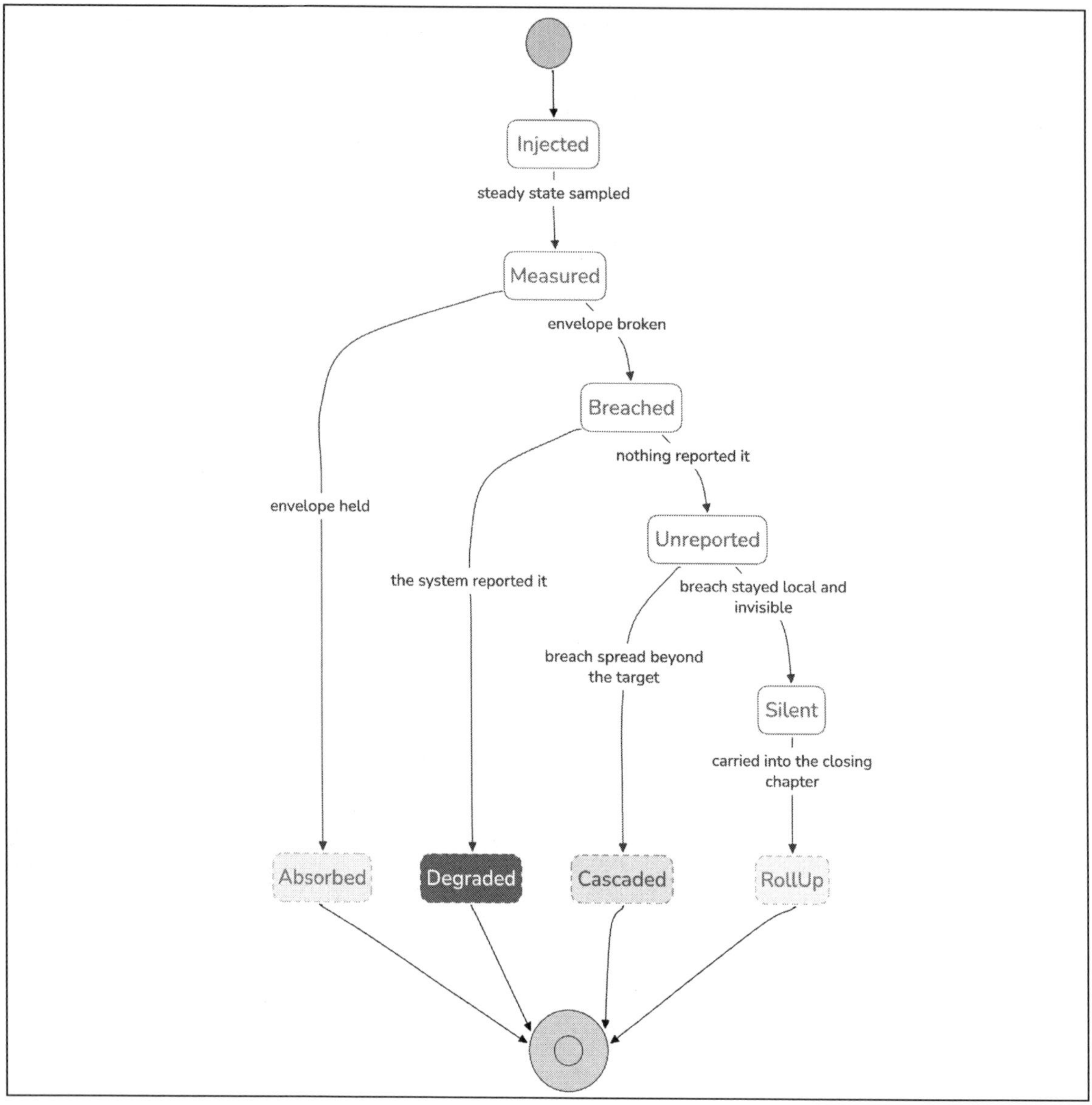

We allow four words only, with no synonyms and no fifth option. Such rigidity looks arbitrary until we try to fill a table without it, at which point every result becomes partially something. Should a result refuse to fit one of the four, our steady state definition is too vague. The correct fix belongs in Chapter 2 rather than in a new word. We also expect roughly one third of all rows across the book to land on silent. Anything much lower suggests our experiments were too gentle to reach the interesting failures.

A single habit makes the vocabulary stick, and we adopt it from the very first experiment. Whoever runs the experiment writes the verdict before hearing anyone else's opinion, then commits it to the results file immediately. Any debate about that verdict happens afterwards, with the original entry preserved. Such discipline sounds bureaucratic for a two-person team, though it pays off the moment the practice spreads.

Mapping Failure Surface

Creating HelpMate Working Repository

We can now put something on disk, which makes everything ahead reproducible. Every artefact we produce lives in one repository, and we create it now so that later chapters stay free of setup noise. For now, we need only four working areas to cover everything the practice requires.

Our first step is to create a working directory and its skeleton as below:

```
mkdir -p ~/helpmate/{signals,experiments,probes,results}
cd ~/helpmate
git init --quiet
tree -L 1
```

The listing confirms our four working areas, each of which fills up as we progress.

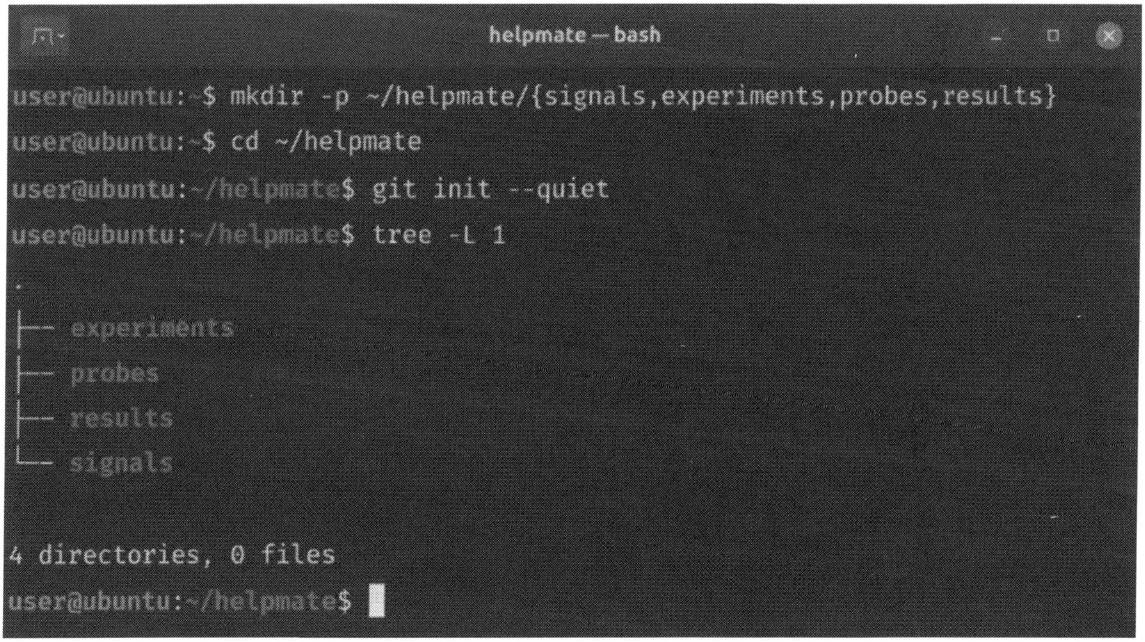

Each directory carries a single responsibility. Our **`signals`** directory holds steady state definitions, one file per service. The **`experiments`** directory will collect Litmus and Chaos Mesh manifests as soon as our cluster exists. Our probe scripts live in **`probes`**, where each one decides pass or fail for a single run. Finally, **`results`** receive one record per experiment, which becomes the raw material for every finding table we publish. These four directories may look sparse today, though by the final chapter the tree describes our entire practice in a form somebody else can clone.

Declaring Signals We Intend to Watch

A single file matters more than the rest, so we write it before anything else. Our signals file names every measurement we intend to defend, organised by the layers we set out earlier. We will not populate trustworthy thresholds yet, since Chapter 2 derives them from a held out set rather than from guesswork. What we can fix today is the shape, because a stable shape lets every later chapter add rows without a renegotiated format. Such consistency costs us ten minutes now and saves us a full rewrite later.

Here is what goes into our first signals file at **`signals/helpmate.yaml`**:

```
service: helpmate
schema: 1
thresholds_state: provisional

layers:
  accelerator:
    - signal: tokens_per_second
      floor: 40
      ceiling: null
    - signal: gpu_throttle_seconds_total
      floor: null
      ceiling: 30
  serving:
    - signal: ttft_p99_ms
      floor: null
      ceiling: 900
    - signal: stream_completion_rate
      floor: 0.98
      ceiling: null
  artifact:
    - signal: model_version_drift
      floor: null
      ceiling: 0
    - signal: cold_start_seconds
      floor: null
      ceiling: 120
  retrieval:
    - signal: recall_at_5
      floor: 0.72
      ceiling: null
    - signal: index_age_hours
      floor: null
```

```yaml
      ceiling: 24
  boundary:
    - signal: response_validity
      floor: 0.90
      ceiling: null
    - signal: refusal_rate
      floor: 0.01
      ceiling: 0.12
  agent:
    - signal: tool_call_success
      floor: 0.95
      ceiling: null
    - signal: escalation_rate
      floor: null
      ceiling: 0.15
  training:
    - signal: checkpoint_write_success
      floor: 1.0
      ceiling: null

verdicts:
  - absorbed
  - degraded
  - cascaded
  - silent
```

Every entry carries a floor, a ceiling, or both, rather than a single number. A floor suits signals where higher is better, as with **`recall_at_5`**. We attach a ceiling where lower is better, as with **`ttft_p99_ms`**.

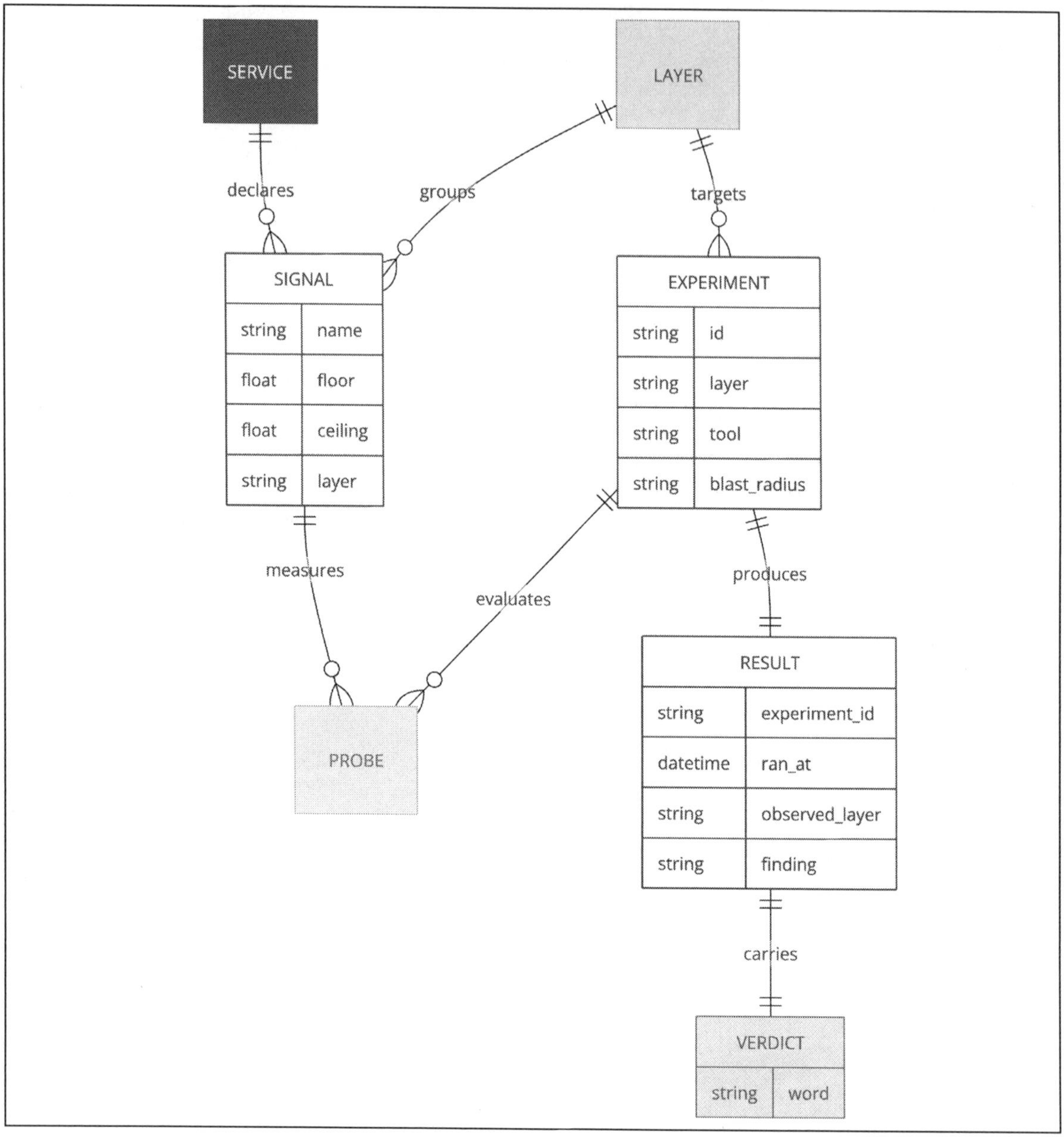

This repository accumulates three record types over time, and their relationships matter more than their contents. A signal definition belongs to exactly one layer and one service. An experiment targets one layer, though it watches many signals at once. A result belongs to one experiment and carries exactly one verdict. Once those relationships hold consistently, we can query months of history and produce any findings table on demand. None of that model requires a database today, since flat files inside **`results`** serve us perfectly well.

Building Coverage Map

The chapter closes with one exercise, and it produces the map we carry forward. We take each layer from our taxonomy, list the failure modes we can imagine, and then mark two columns honestly. The first column asks whether our current monitoring would catch that mode. Our second column asks whether the evaluation suite would catch it. Most teams find the same pattern on first attempt, where the lower layers show plenty of coverage and the upper layers show almost none. That asymmetry is the reason this book exists.

Layer	**Failure mode**	**Monitoring catches it**	**Evaluation catches it**
Accelerator	Power throttling under thermal load	Partly	No
Accelerator	Correctable ECC accumulation	No	No
Serving	KV cache exhaustion under batching	Partly	No
Serving	Response truncated mid stream	No	No
Artifact	Model version changed silently	No	No
Artifact	Weights file partially read	No	No
Retrieval	Index stale beyond tolerance	No	No
Retrieval	Embedding version skew	No	No
Boundary	Schema valid, semantically wrong	No	Partly
Boundary	Fallback model engaged quietly	No	No
Agent	Tool returns plausible wrong data	No	No
Agent	Retry loop inflates token spend	Partly	No
Training	Resumed run diverges from original	No	Partly

We should fill this table for our own stack before moving on, and honesty matters more than completeness. A row marked yes because somebody once built a dashboard does not qualify, unless an alert fires and reaches a named person. Every no in the right-hand columns marks a chapter we now have reason to read carefully. In the next chapter, we turn the sparse right-hand side of this map into measurable definitions, after which we finally earn the right to inject anything at all.

Summary

We began with a single observation, that the binary model of failure stops working once a language model enters our request path. That conclusion rested on four properties, namely probabilistic output, a fuzzy baseline, slow compounding decay, and confident wrongness. We then spent real time with HelpMate, from its hundred and twenty support agents down to the four stateful dependencies behind its services. Our worked scenario showed six weeks of retrieval decay passing unnoticed while every infrastructure signal stayed nominal.

We also organised the architecture into seven layers and fixed the vocabulary we use from here onward, where absorbed, degraded, cascaded, and silent cover every possible outcome. That last word carries the weight of the book, since it names the case, our dashboards cannot see. On disk, we started the **`helpmate`** repository and wrote our first signals file, which pins the shape of every steady state definition to come. In the next chapter, we fill that shape with thresholds derived from a held-out set.

CHAPTER 2

STEADY STATE FOR PROBABILISTIC SYSTEM

None of the chapters ahead has meaning without the work in this one. We cannot inject a fault and claim a result until we have written down what correct behaviour looks like. In the previous chapter, we were left with a signals file full of provisional numbers and a coverage map full of gaps. Both of those artefacts now need real values, derived from evidence rather than from opinion. Every experiment in the book measures against what we settle here.

Across this chapter, we will assemble a golden set, capture a baseline from it, and reduce that capture to one number per signal. We then derive envelopes from those numbers using bootstrap bounds combined with deliberate human slack. Along the way, we meet the overconfidence trap that makes refusal rate a two-sided measurement. Our final section writes an experiment specification, validates it before any cluster sees it, and fixes the abort conditions. By the close, we hold a runnable steady state definition and one experiment ready to schedule.

Steady State While Output Not Still

From Single Thresholds to Envelopes

A threshold works beautifully for a signal with one correct value. Our disk either fills or it does not, and ninety percent utilisation means the same thing every Tuesday. Once we measure something that varies legitimately, the single threshold begins to lie in both directions. A tight setting drowns us in alerts caused by ordinary Monday morning traffic. A loose setting lets us sleep through a genuine collapse. Neither failure mode improves with a cleverer number, because the problem lives in the shape of the measurement rather than in its value.

An envelope replaces that single number with a permitted region. We declare a floor, a ceiling, or both, and any value inside the region counts as normal operation. Our **`recall_at_5`** measurement carries only a floor, since retrieval quality above expectation harms nobody. The time to first token carries only a ceiling, for the mirror reason. A handful of measurements need both, and those turn out to be the most informative ones in the whole file. Our envelopes also give us arithmetic that a threshold cannot supply. When a value falls outside its region, we can express how far outside as a signed distance rather than as a boolean. That distance tells us whether we brushed the boundary or drove through it at speed. Over many experiments, the distribution of breach distances shows which signals sit uncomfortably close to their limits during ordinary operation. We treat those signals as fragile and widen them deliberately, rather than pretending the near misses never happened.

Separating Ordinary Variance from Real Drift

Every measurement we take contains two different sources of movement:

1. The first source is sampling noise, which arises because we measured four hundred requests rather than every request ever served. Our estimate would land somewhere slightly different had we sampled on a different afternoon.

2. The second source is genuine change in the system, where the underlying behaviour actually moved.

A confusion between the two produces either constant false alarms or a comfortable blindness, and no amount of dashboard polish resolves it. We separate them cleanly enough for our purposes with bootstrap resampling. We draw many synthetic samples from our observed data, compute the statistic on each one, and observe how much the answer wobbles. A narrow spread tells us the estimate is precise, so a small movement in production means something real. A wide spread tells us the opposite, and we should widen the envelope accordingly. The technique requires no heavy machinery, since a few thousand resamples finish in under a second on any laptop.

A warning belongs here before we write code. Our bootstrap bounds describe how precisely we measured the current behaviour, and they say nothing whatsoever about how much that behaviour may legitimately vary next week. A sample of four hundred requests produces a very tight interval around the mean, tight enough that a perfectly healthy Thursday would breach it. We therefore treat those bounds as a starting point and add human slack on top. That slack encodes our tolerance for false alarms, which is a judgement call rather than a calculation.

Building Golden Set

What Belongs Inside Golden Set?

Our golden set is a fixed collection of support questions with known correct responses. Every question inside it must satisfy three conditions before we admit it. The question has to reflect traffic we actually receive, so we sample from real ticket history rather than inventing plausible sounding queries. The correct response has to be settled by somebody with authority, which for HelpMate means a senior support lead rather than the engineer who wrote the retrieval code. Finally, the question must never appear in any training or fine tuning corpus. That third condition causes more trouble than the first two combined. Many teams build a set from resolved tickets, then later fine tune on resolved tickets, and the set quietly stops measuring anything. We defend against the collision by tagging every golden question in Postgres with an exclusion flag, and by filtering that flag inside the training data export. Such plumbing feels tedious on the day we build it. Months later, the same plumbing is the only reason our numbers still mean something.

The size of the set matters less than most teams expect. A set of four hundred questions gives us enough statistical resolution for the signals we care about, and it stays cheap enough to run several times a day. We weight the composition toward the query families that carry business risk, so settlement failures and refund windows receive heavier representation than general product questions. Roughly, one tenth of the set consists of questions HelpMate genuinely should refuse, because a set containing only answerable questions cannot detect overconfidence at all.

Capturing Baseline before Cluster Exists

We face an ordering problem worth naming directly. Our lab does not exist yet, since the next chapter builds it, and yet steady state has to come first. Fortunately, the two concerns separate cleanly. Every number we need can be computed from a capture file, which holds one record per served request. A team with a running system exports that file from their existing telemetry, while the rest of us synthesize one locally. Either path produces identical downstream code, so nothing here needs rewriting once real traffic arrives.

So, in the file **`probes/capture.py`**, we will write one JSON object per line, one line per request, with no nesting beyond scalars:

```
cd ~/helpmate
python3 -m pip install --user pyyaml
touch probes/__init__.py
"""Synthesize capture files so the probes run before any cluster
exists."""
from __future__ import annotations

import argparse
import json
import random
from pathlib import Path

PROFILES = {
    "healthy": {"recall_centre": 0.81, "refusal_p": 0.045,
"headroom": 1.00},
    "stale": {"recall_centre": 0.64, "refusal_p": 0.018,
"headroom": 1.00},
    "throttled": {"recall_centre": 0.81, "refusal_p": 0.045,
"headroom": 0.87},
    "starved": {"recall_centre": 0.81, "refusal_p": 0.045,
"headroom": 0.55},
    "drained": {"recall_centre": 0.70, "refusal_p": 0.045,
"headroom": 1.00},
}


def one_record(rng: random.Random, index: int, profile: dict) ->
dict:
    headroom = profile["headroom"]
    recall = min(1.0, max(0.0, rng.gauss(profile["recall_centre"],
0.11)))
    refused = rng.random() < profile["refusal_p"]
    overridden = (not refused) and rng.random() < (0.04 + 0.55 *
max(0.0, 0.80 - recall))
    planned = rng.choice([0, 0, 1, 2, 3])
    # Below roughly two thirds of nominal compute, streams start
```

```
timing out.
    complete_p = 0.996 if headroom >= 0.65 else 0.996 - (0.65 -
headroom) * 1.4
    return {
        "query_id": f"q{index:05d}",
        "ttft_ms": round(rng.lognormvariate(5.72, 0.34) / headroom,
1),
        "tokens_per_second": round(rng.gauss(58.0, 6.5) * headroom,
2),
        "recall_at_5": round(recall, 4),
        "refused": refused,
        "overridden": overridden,
        "escalated": overridden and rng.random() < 0.28,
        "stream_complete": rng.random() < complete_p,
        "tool_calls_planned": planned,
        "tool_calls_ok": planned - (1 if planned and rng.random() <
0.02 else 0),
    }


def main() -> None:
    parser = argparse.ArgumentParser(description="Write a HelpMate
capture file")
    parser.add_argument("--profile", choices=sorted(PROFILES),
default="healthy")
    parser.add_argument("--records", type=int, default=400)
    parser.add_argument("--seed", type=int, default=11)
    args = parser.parse_args()

    rng = random.Random(args.seed)
    profile = PROFILES[args.profile]
    out = Path(f"results/{args.profile}-capture.jsonl")
    out.parent.mkdir(parents=True, exist_ok=True)
    with out.open("w", encoding="utf-8") as handle:
        for index in range(args.records):
            handle.write(json.dumps(one_record(rng, index,
profile)) + "\n")
    print(f"wrote {out} with {args.records} records")


if __name__ == "__main__":
    main()
```

At this stage, two profiles matter most, and the second matters as much as the first. Our **`healthy`** profile reproduces HelpMate on a normal day. The **`stale`** profile reproduces the same system after the index ages, with retrieval quality lowered and refusals made rarer. We will use the pair as a controlled before and after, which lets us validate the whole measurement chain before we ever inject a real fault.

So now, we will generate both captures:

```
python3 -m probes.capture --profile healthy
python3 -m probes.capture --profile stale
```

Here, both commands report the path they wrote along with the number of records.

```
wrote results/healthy-capture.jsonl with 400 records
wrote results/stale-capture.jsonl with 400 records
```

Keeping Set Honest Over Time

A golden set decays the moment we stop maintaining it. The product changes, new features arrive, and questions that were correct in March become wrong by September. We therefore schedule a quarterly review where a support lead re-validates every response and retires anything obsolete. A retired question moves to an archive file rather than vanishing, so historical comparisons remain interpretable. Roughly one tenth of the set turns over each quarter in our experience, which is manageable when planned and painful when deferred for a year.

Another habit protects the set from a subtler failure. We record the date each question entered the set and the date each correct response was last confirmed. Any question whose confirmation date drifts past twelve months gets flagged automatically during the reduction step. Such flagging costs nothing and prevents the slow rot where nobody can remember whether a given response was ever authoritative. Our trust in the baseline is the foundation for trust in every verdict we publish afterwards.

Choosing Signals

Signals with Named Owner

The metrics that describe model quality and the signals that describe operation answer different questions, and only one kind belongs in our envelope file. A perplexity score tells a machine learning engineer something during model selection. That same score tells the on call engineer at two in the morning absolutely nothing actionable. Our filter is therefore blunt. Any signal we declare must have a named human who would change their behaviour in response to it moving, and a written first action they would take.

That filter applied to HelpMate produces a shorter list than we expected. The override rate passes immediately, because the support operations lead owns it and their first action involves sampling the overridden drafts. The recall at five measurement passes too, owned by the retrieval engineer, whose first action is a re-index. There are several tempting candidates that fail, including average response length and token entropy, since nobody could name what they would do differently.

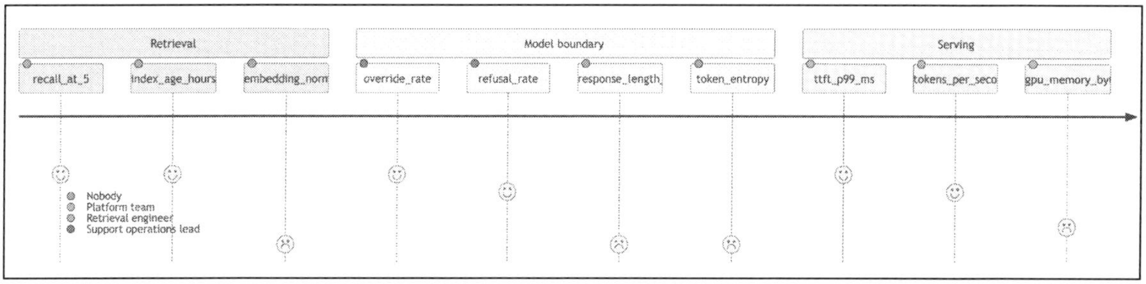

In that view, three signals scored a single point, and we deleted all three from the file. Such deletion feels wasteful, since collecting them costs almost nothing. Every undeleted signal carries an ongoing tax, however, because somebody must interpret it during every experiment review for the rest of the programme. A file of eight meaningful signals produces better decisions than a file of thirty, where twenty-two of them get skipped by everyone reading the results.

Overconfidence Trap in Two Sided Signals

The refusal rate deserves particular attention, since it behaves unlike anything else in our file. Most teams treat refusals as pure friction and drive the number toward zero. A refusal rate approaching zero means our model never admits ignorance, which is not a strength. When retrieval degrades and the model keeps producing confident output from irrelevant context, the refusal rate falls at exactly the moment quality collapses.

We therefore declare refusal rate with both a floor and a ceiling. The ceiling catches the obvious failure where retrieval breaks loudly and the system gives up too often. The floor catches the dangerous failure where the system stops giving up at all. Our stale profile demonstrates the effect precisely, since it lowers refusal probability while lowering retrieval quality. Both movements happen together in real systems, for the straightforward reason that a model with poor context still has plenty of tokens available. Our golden set has to contain unanswerable questions, or the floor becomes meaningless. Should every question in the set have a good response available, a healthy system would refuse almost nothing and our floor would sit at zero. We reserve roughly forty of the four hundred slots for questions where the correct behaviour involves declining. Between them, those forty questions do more work in detecting silent degradation than the other three hundred and sixty combined.

Deriving Envelopes from Baseline

Bootstrap Bounds and Human Slack

We can now build the arithmetic that turns a capture into envelopes. The load falls on two modules, where the first holds envelope mechanics and the second reduces raw records into signal values. Their separation matters, because Chapter 3 replaces the reduction step with live cluster queries while leaving the envelope mechanics untouched. Our percentile helper uses linear interpolation between ranks, which matches what Prometheus reports and avoids an awkward mismatch later.

In **probes/envelope.py** as shown below, we will write the envelope module:

```
"""Envelope loading and breach arithmetic for HelpMate steady
state."""
from __future__ import annotations

import math
import random
from dataclasses import dataclass
from pathlib import Path
from typing import Callable, Sequence

import yaml


@dataclass(frozen=True)
class Envelope:
    signal: str
    layer: str
    floor: float | None
    ceiling: float | None

    def holds(self, value: float) -> bool:
        if self.floor is not None and value < self.floor:
            return False
        if self.ceiling is not None and value > self.ceiling:
            return False
        return True

    def breach(self, value: float) -> float:
        if self.floor is not None and value < self.floor:
            return round(value - self.floor, 6)
        if self.ceiling is not None and value > self.ceiling:
            return round(value - self.ceiling, 6)
        return 0.0


def load_envelopes(path: Path) -> dict[str, Envelope]:
    spec = yaml.safe_load(path.read_text(encoding="utf-8"))
    envelopes: dict[str, Envelope] = {}
    for layer, entries in spec["layers"].items():
```

```
        for entry in entries:
            envelopes[entry["signal"]] = Envelope(
                signal=entry["signal"],
                layer=layer,
                floor=entry.get("floor"),
                ceiling=entry.get("ceiling"),
            )
    return envelopes


def percentile(values: Sequence[float], p: float) -> float:
    ordered = sorted(values)
    if not ordered:
        raise ValueError("percentile of an empty sample")
    rank = (len(ordered) - 1) * (p / 100.0)
    low, high = math.floor(rank), math.ceil(rank)
    if low == high:
        return float(ordered[low])
    weight = rank - low
    return ordered[low] * (1.0 - weight) + ordered[high] * weight


def bootstrap_bounds(
    values: Sequence[float],
    statistic: Callable[[Sequence[float]], float],
    iterations: int = 2000,
    seed: int = 7,
) -> tuple[float, float]:
    rng = random.Random(seed)
    size = len(values)
    draws = []
    for _ in range(iterations):
        resample = [values[rng.randrange(size)] for _ in
range(size)]
        draws.append(statistic(resample))
    return percentile(draws, 2.5), percentile(draws, 97.5)
```

Next, we will add the reduction module at **probes/reduce.py**:

```
"""Reduce a capture file to exactly one value per declared
signal."""
from __future__ import annotations

import json
from pathlib import Path
from statistics import fmean
```

```
from typing import Sequence

from probes.envelope import percentile


def read_capture(path: Path) -> list[dict]:
    with path.open(encoding="utf-8") as handle:
        return [json.loads(line) for line in handle if
line.strip()]


def reduce_signals(records: Sequence[dict]) -> dict[str, float]:
    submitted = len(records)
    if submitted == 0:
        raise ValueError("capture file holds no records")
    records = [r for r in records if r.get("admitted", True)]
    total = len(records) or 1
    tooled = [r for r in records if r["tool_calls_planned"] > 0]
    clean = [r for r in tooled if r["tool_calls_ok"] ==
r["tool_calls_planned"]]
    served = [r for r in records if not r["refused"]] or records
    values = {
        "ttft_p99_ms": round(percentile([r["ttft_ms"] for r in
records], 99), 1),
        "tokens_per_second": round(fmean(r["tokens_per_second"] for
r in records), 2),
        "recall_at_5": round(fmean(r["recall_at_5"] for r in
records), 4),
        "refusal_rate": round(sum(r["refused"] for r in records) /
total, 4),
        "override_rate": round(sum(r["overridden"] for r in served)
/ len(served), 4),
        "escalation_rate": round(sum(r["escalated"] for r in
records) / total, 4),
        "stream_completion_rate": round(
            sum(r["stream_complete"] for r in records) / total, 4
        ),
        "tool_call_success": round(len(clean) / len(tooled), 4) if
tooled else 1.0,
    }
    return values
```

The override rate divides by served requests rather than by all requests. A refused request never produced a draft, so the agent had nothing to override, and including it would dilute the signal exactly when refusals rise. The small decisions of that kind determine whether a measurement stays interpretable under stress. Hence, we record the reasoning in a comment beside every non obvious denominator, since the person debugging a strange result six months from now will otherwise assume a bug.

Committing Derived Envelopes

Our derivation script combines the bootstrap bounds with a slack file that we maintain by hand. A separation between the two makes the judgement visible instead of burying it inside a formula. A reviewer can see the statistical bound, see the slack we added, and argue with the second number without touching the first. We resisted an automatic margin rule, because no single rule behaves sensibly across a latency measured in hundreds of milliseconds and a rate bounded at one.

So our slack values get declared at **probes/slack.yaml** like this:

```
ttft_p99_ms: 120.0
tokens_per_second: 6.0
recall_at_5: 0.06
refusal_rate: 0.02
override_rate: 0.02
escalation_rate: 0.03
stream_completion_rate: 0.01
tool_call_success: 0.02
```

And then, we will write the derivation script at **probes/derive.py**:

```
"""Propose floors and ceilings from a healthy capture, using
bootstrap bounds."""
from __future__ import annotations

import argparse
from pathlib import Path
from statistics import fmean

import yaml

from probes.envelope import bootstrap_bounds, percentile
from probes.reduce import read_capture

DIRECTION = {
    "ttft_p99_ms": "ceiling",
    "tokens_per_second": "floor",
    "recall_at_5": "floor",
    "refusal_rate": "both",
    "override_rate": "ceiling",
    "escalation_rate": "ceiling",
    "stream_completion_rate": "floor",
```

```
    "tool_call_success": "floor",
}

SAMPLERS = {
    "ttft_p99_ms": lambda rs: [r["ttft_ms"] for r in rs],
    "tokens_per_second": lambda rs: [r["tokens_per_second"] for r
in rs],
    "recall_at_5": lambda rs: [r["recall_at_5"] for r in rs],
    "refusal_rate": lambda rs: [float(r["refused"]) for r in rs],
    "override_rate": lambda rs: [float(r["overridden"]) for r in
rs],
    "escalation_rate": lambda rs: [float(r["escalated"]) for r in
rs],
    "stream_completion_rate": lambda rs:
[float(r["stream_complete"]) for r in rs],
    "tool_call_success": lambda rs: [
        1.0 if r["tool_calls_ok"] == r["tool_calls_planned"] else
0.0
        for r in rs
        if r["tool_calls_planned"] > 0
    ],
}

STATISTIC = {"ttft_p99_ms": lambda xs: percentile(xs, 99)}


def main() -> None:
    parser = argparse.ArgumentParser(description="Propose envelopes
from a capture")
    parser.add_argument("--capture", default="results/healthy-
capture.jsonl")
    parser.add_argument("--slack", default="probes/slack.yaml")
    args = parser.parse_args()

    records = read_capture(Path(args.capture))
    slack =
yaml.safe_load(Path(args.slack).read_text(encoding="utf-8"))

print(f"{'signal':<24}{'lo95':>10}{'hi95':>10}{'floor':>10}{'ceilin
g':>10}")
    print("-" * 64)
    for name, sampler in SAMPLERS.items():
        if name not in slack:
            continue
        statistic = STATISTIC.get(name, fmean)
        low, high = bootstrap_bounds(sampler(records), statistic)
```

```
        room = slack[name]
        direction = DIRECTION[name]
        floor = ceiling = None
        if direction in ("floor", "both"):
            floor = round(low - room, 4)
        if direction in ("ceiling", "both"):
            ceiling = round(high + room, 4)
        show = lambda v: "-" if v is None else f"{v}"
        print(
            f"{name:<24}{round(low, 4):>10}{round(high, 4):>10}"
            f"{show(floor):>10}{show(ceiling):>10}"
        )


if __name__ == "__main__":
    main()
```

```
python3 -m probes.derive
```

This gives four columns, showing the bootstrap interval alongside the envelope we would commit.

```
signal                          lo95      hi95     floor   ceiling
------------------------------------------------------------------
ttft_p99_ms                    614.6     713.9         -     833.9
tokens_per_second            57.2346   58.5288   51.2346         -
recall_at_5                    0.793    0.8137     0.733         -
refusal_rate                    0.03    0.0725      0.01    0.0925
override_rate                  0.025     0.065         -     0.085
escalation_rate                0.005      0.03         -      0.06
stream_completion_rate        0.9925       1.0    0.9825         -
tool_call_success             0.9504    0.9917    0.9304         -
```

If you notice it clearly, it is a simple comparison of the intervals against the final bounds makes the value of slack obvious. Our bootstrap places recall between 0.793 and 0.8137, an interval so tight that any ordinary fluctuation would breach it. A further six percentage points of slack move the floor to 0.733, which tolerates a normal bad afternoon while still catching the stale index scenario. We round these numbers into **signals/helpmate.yaml**, bump the schema version to two, and change **thresholds_state** from provisional to derived.

Our checking script closes the loop by evaluating any capture against the committed file. So now, we will write it at **probes/check.py**:

```
"""Evaluate one capture against the declared envelopes and return a
verdict."""
from __future__ import annotations
```

```
import argparse
from pathlib import Path

from probes.envelope import Envelope, load_envelopes
from probes.reduce import read_capture, reduce_signals


def report(values: dict[str, float], envelopes: dict[str,
Envelope]) -> list[str]:
    breached: list[str] = []
    print(f"{'signal':<24}{'value':>10}{'floor':>10}{'ceiling':>10}
status")
    print("-" * 66)
    for name in sorted(values):
        value = values[name]
        env = envelopes.get(name)
        if env is None:
            print(f"{name:<24}{value:>10}{'-':>10}{'-':>10}
undeclared")
            continue
        floor = "-" if env.floor is None else f"{env.floor}"
        ceiling = "-" if env.ceiling is None else f"{env.ceiling}"
        if env.holds(value):
            status = "inside"
        else:
            status = f"BREACH {env.breach(value):+}"
            breached.append(name)
        print(f"{name:<24}{value:>10}{floor:>10}{ceiling:>10}
{status}")
    return breached


def main() -> None:
    parser = argparse.ArgumentParser(description="Check a capture
against signals")
    parser.add_argument("--capture", default="results/healthy-
capture.jsonl")
    parser.add_argument("--signals",
default="signals/helpmate.yaml")
    args = parser.parse_args()

    records = read_capture(Path(args.capture))
    values = reduce_signals(records)
    envelopes = load_envelopes(Path(args.signals))
    breached = report(values, envelopes)
    pending = sorted(set(envelopes) - set(values))
```

```
    print("-" * 66)
    print(f"{len(records)} records, {len(breached)} breach(es),
{len(pending)} not yet captured")
    if breached:
        print("breached:", ", ".join(breached))
    if pending:
        print("awaiting a live cluster:", ", ".join(pending))
    raise SystemExit(1 if breached else 0)


if __name__ == "__main__":
    main()
```

After this, we then run the check against our healthy capture, so it can confirm the envelopes admit normal behaviour.

```
python3 -m probes.check --capture results/healthy-capture.jsonl
```

In the following output, we can notice that every declared signal sits inside its region, and six signals wait for a cluster that does not exist yet.

```
signal                          value      floor    ceiling  status
------------------------------------------------------------------
escalation_rate                0.0175          -       0.06  inside
override_rate                  0.0474          -      0.085  inside
recall_at_5                    0.8035      0.733          -  inside
refusal_rate                     0.05       0.01     0.0925  inside
stream_completion_rate         0.9975     0.9825          -  inside
tokens_per_second                57.9      51.23          -  inside
tool_call_success              0.9711     0.9304          -  inside
ttft_p99_ms                     652.7          -      833.9  inside
------------------------------------------------------------------
400 records, 0 breach(es), 6 not yet captured
awaiting a live cluster: checkpoint_write_success,
cold_start_seconds, gpu_throttle_seconds_total, index_age_hours,
model_version_drift, response_validity
```

The same check against the stale capture produces the result the whole book exists to demonstrate.

```
python3 -m probes.check --capture results/stale-capture.jsonl
```

Here, there are two quality signals that breach, while every infrastructure signal holds perfectly steady.

```
signal                        value      floor    ceiling   status
------------------------------------------------------------------
escalation_rate                0.03          -       0.06   inside
override_rate                0.1253          -      0.085   BREACH
+0.0403
recall_at_5                  0.6289      0.733          -   BREACH -
0.1041
refusal_rate                 0.0225       0.01     0.0925   inside
stream_completion_rate       0.9975     0.9825          -   inside
tokens_per_second             58.09      51.23          -   inside
tool_call_success            0.9675     0.9304          -   inside
ttft_p99_ms                   673.7          -      833.9   inside
------------------------------------------------------------------
400 records, 2 breach(es), 6 not yet captured
breached: override_rate, recall_at_5
```

The refusal rate across those two runs repays a careful look. Our healthy capture refused five percent of requests, while the stale capture refused only two and a quarter percent. The quality fell and the system became more willing to respond, exactly as the overconfidence trap predicts. That movement stayed inside our envelope on this occasion, though it sat within a whisker of the floor. Any team watching refusals with a ceiling alone would have recorded the drop as progress.

Designing Safe Experiment

Hypothesis, Blast Radius, and Exclusion Zones

An experiment specification records four things that a script cannot:

1. The first is a falsifiable hypothesis, written as a prediction about signal movement rather than as a description of what we will break.
2. Our second element is the watch list, naming every signal we sample during the run.
3. The third is blast radius, expressed as a namespace, a traffic fraction, and a number of affected replicas. And,
4. The fourth covers exclusion zones, listing components the experiment must never touch under any circumstance.

Our exclusion zones deserve more thought than teams usually give them. We protect **helpmate-gateway** because losing it removes our ability to observe anything at all. Our Postgres instance receives the same protection, since it holds the override records that constitute our quality ground truth. The loss of our measurement apparatus during a run turns a controlled experiment into an ordinary outage with extra paperwork. Any component whose failure would blind us belongs on that list, regardless of how interesting breaking it might seem.

Here's what our first experiment looks like at **experiments/exp-001-index-staleness.yaml**:

```yaml
id: exp-001-index-staleness
service: helpmate
injection_layer: retrieval
observation_layer: boundary
tool: byoc

hypothesis: >
  Once the Qdrant index ages beyond 72 hours, recall_at_5 falls
below its
  floor and override_rate rises above its ceiling within the same
window,
  while every serving and accelerator signal stays inside its
envelope.

watch:
  - recall_at_5
  - override_rate
  - refusal_rate
  - escalation_rate
  - ttft_p99_ms
  - tokens_per_second
  - stream_completion_rate

blast_radius:
  namespace: helpmate-staging
  traffic_fraction: 0.10
  replicas_affected: 1

exclusion_zones:
  - helpmate-gateway
  - postgres

gating:
  min_error_budget_remaining: 0.30
  baseline_max_age_hours: 24
  require_named_operator: true

abort_when:
  - signal: override_rate
    above: 0.20
  - signal: escalation_rate
    above: 0.12
```

```yaml
  - signal: ttft_p99_ms
    above: 1500

windows:
  baseline_minutes: 15
  injection_minutes: 20
  recovery_minutes: 10

kill_switch: probes/abort.sh
```

In the above yaml, the specification records what we predict, what we will watch, how far the blast reaches, and what the run must never touch, so that a disagreement afterwards can be settled against a document written before anybody knew the answer. Our next section adds the gates that decide whether this file is allowed to become a running experiment at all.

Gating, Abort Conditions, and Kill Switch

A written specification passes three gates before it becomes a running experiment:

1. Our error budget gate refuses to proceed when less than thirty percent of the monthly budget remains, because a system already consuming its reliability headroom should not receive additional stress.
2. The baseline age gate refuses when our last healthy capture is older than twenty four hours, since comparing against a stale baseline produces meaningless deltas.
3. Finally, the operator gate requires a named human who is watching, which sounds bureaucratic until the first time somebody schedules a run over a holiday weekend.

An abort condition differs from an envelope breach in an important way. A breach is the result we are looking for, so breaching an envelope never stops the run. An abort threshold sits considerably further out, at the point where continuing would harm real users rather than teach us something. Our override rate envelope sits at 0.085 while the abort fires at 0.20, which leaves generous room to observe degradation before we intervene. With those two numbers set too close together, an experiment aborts before it reveals anything.

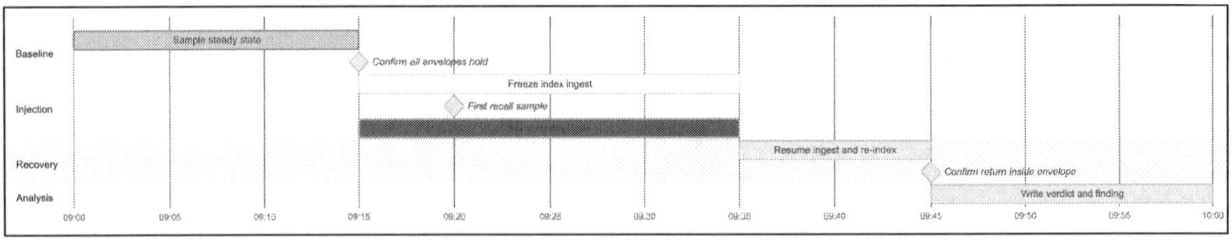

Our kill switch has one job, which involves ending the experiment faster than any human can reason about it. We keep it as a single script requiring one argument, so that a stressed engineer at midnight has nothing to remember. The script deletes the chaos resource, restarts the affected deployment, and appends a timestamped line to an abort log. It consults no configuration and asks for no confirmation. Any kill switch that requires thought during an incident is not a kill switch.

The given below is the abort script, saved in **probes/abort.sh**:

```
#!/usr/bin/env bash
# Single command that ends any running experiment immediately.
set -euo pipefail
EXPERIMENT="${1:?usage: abort.sh <experiment-id>}"
echo "$(date -Is) aborting ${EXPERIMENT}" | tee -a
results/abort.log
kubectl -n helpmate-staging delete chaosengine "${EXPERIMENT}" --
ignore-not-found
kubectl -n helpmate-staging rollout restart deploy/helpmate-
retriever
echo "$(date -Is) abort complete for ${EXPERIMENT}" | tee -a
results/abort.log
```

If we precisely look at the script, we can notice that, it reads no configuration, asks for no confirmation, and takes exactly one argument. And it is because a stressed engineer at midnight should have nothing to remember and nothing to look up. Our own rule is that the kill switch gets exercised on the day it is written and again before every game day, on the grounds that an untested abort path is an assumption rather than a control.

Pre-flight Gate

A final script refuses to let a malformed specification reach a cluster. Our validator checks that every required key exists, that every watched signal has a declared envelope, and that every abort signal appears on the watch list. That last check catches a mistake teams make constantly, where an abort condition references a signal nobody is sampling. Such a condition can never fire, and the experiment runs with no upper guard while everyone believes it is protected.

We will quickly look at writing the validator in **probes/validate_experiment.py**:

```
"""Reject an experiment spec before it ever reaches a cluster."""
from __future__ import annotations

import argparse
from pathlib import Path

import yaml

from probes.envelope import load_envelopes

REQUIRED = {
    "id", "service", "injection_layer", "observation_layer",
```

```
"tool", "hypothesis",
    "watch", "blast_radius", "exclusion_zones", "gating",
"abort_when",
    "windows", "kill_switch",
}


def validate(spec: dict, envelopes: dict) -> list[str]:
    problems = [f"missing key '{key}'" for key in sorted(REQUIRED -
set(spec))]
    for name in spec.get("watch", []):
        if name not in envelopes:
            problems.append(f"watched signal '{name}' has no
declared envelope")
    for rule in spec.get("abort_when", []):
        if rule["signal"] not in spec.get("watch", []):
            problems.append(f"abort signal '{rule['signal']}' is
not watched")
    if not spec.get("exclusion_zones"):
        problems.append("exclusion_zones must name at least one
protected component")
    windows = spec.get("windows", {})
    if windows.get("baseline_minutes", 0) < 10:
        problems.append("baseline_minutes below the 10 minute
minimum")
    return problems


def main() -> None:
    parser = argparse.ArgumentParser(description="Validate an
experiment spec")
    parser.add_argument("spec")
    parser.add_argument("--signals",
default="signals/helpmate.yaml")
    args = parser.parse_args()

    spec = yaml.safe_load(Path(args.spec).read_text(encoding="utf-
8"))
    problems = validate(spec, load_envelopes(Path(args.signals)))
    if problems:
        for problem in problems:
            print(f"reject: {problem}")
        raise SystemExit(1)
    print(f"accept: {spec['id']} is safe to schedule")
```

```
if __name__ == "__main__":
    main()
```

Our specification passes cleanly, which means it may proceed once the cluster exists.

```
python3 -m probes.validate_experiment experiments/exp-001-index-staleness.yaml
```

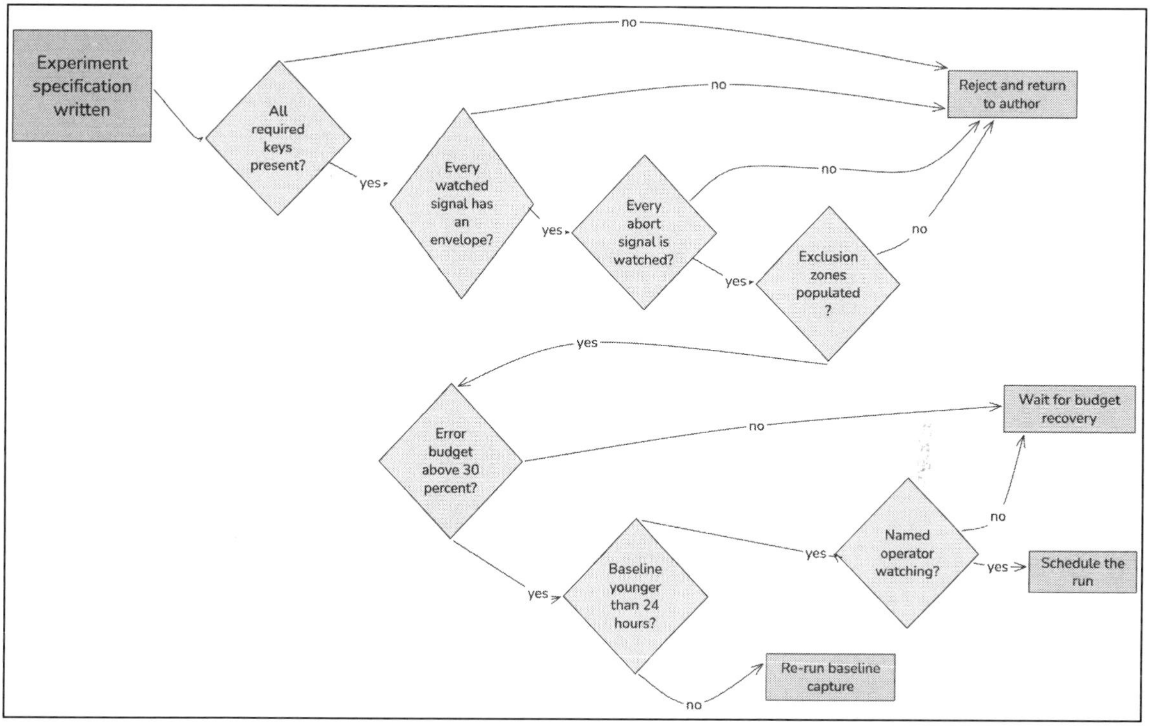

Every gate in the above sequence exists because somebody once skipped it and regretted the outcome. We run the validator inside continuous integration as well as by hand, so a specification cannot reach the experiments directory without passing. In Chapter 3 we build the cluster this specification targets, install the three tools we settled on, and connect our reduction step to live telemetry rather than to a capture file. None of the envelope arithmetic changes at that point, which is precisely why we built it first.

Summary

We turned an empty signals file into a working steady state definition. Our envelope model replaced single thresholds with permitted regions, gave us signed breach distances, and handled the two-sided case that pure ceilings cannot express. We built a golden set of four hundred questions, reserved forty slots for questions HelpMate should refuse, and captured both a healthy and a stale profile. Our bootstrap bounds then supplied statistical precision, while a hand maintained slack file supplied our tolerance for false alarms.

We ran the checker against both captures, which produced the demonstration that justifies the whole practice. Our retrieval quality and override rate breached their envelopes, refusal rate quietly fell toward its floor, and every serving signal stayed comfortably inside. We closed by writing an experiment specification with a falsifiable hypothesis, explicit exclusion zones, three scheduling gates, and abort thresholds set well outside the envelope. Our validator now refuses malformed specifications automatically. In the next chapter, we build the cluster where all of this finally runs against live traffic.

CHAPTER 3

LAB AND THE TOOLCHAIN

In the previous chapter, we ended with a working steady state definition and no system to apply it to. Our envelopes were derived from a capture file, our experiment specification passed validation, and nothing anywhere was actually running. That gap closes now. In this chapter, we will build a three node cluster, deploy HelpMate onto it, install the three tools we settled on, and connect our probes to live telemetry rather than to a file on disk.

Across this chapter, we will create the cluster with kind, package HelpMate as a single small image, and stand up Prometheus with pod discovery. We then install LitmusChaos, Chaos Mesh, and mitmproxy, each with a clearly separated job. Our reduction step gets a second implementation that queries Prometheus while producing identical output. A drift guard follows, which refuses to let probe thresholds diverge from the committed envelopes. By the close, we will have run our first experiment twice and recorded the result.

Sizing Lab against Real System

What We Reproduce, and What We Shrink?

Our production HelpMate handles forty requests per minute across four services and four stateful dependencies. A full scale reproduction would cost more than the exercise is worth. Instead we preserve topology and shrink capacity, since topology determines how faults propagate while capacity only determines how quickly. A three node cluster with two replicas per service reproduces every propagation path in the real system. Anything we learn about how a retriever failure reaches the gateway holds identically at either size. The shrinking must leave three properties intact, and we protect them deliberately. Our service boundaries stay intact, so a fault injected at the retriever cannot reach the gateway except through the network. The separation between nodes stays intact as well, which lets us test node level faults without them accidentally taking the whole cluster. Finally, our metric names stay identical between lab and production, because a probe written against the lab must work unchanged against the real system.

Several things get dropped without regret. We drop authentication, since testing our own token validation teaches us nothing about resilience. The persistent storage for Prometheus disappears too, given that six hours of retention covers any experiment we run. Our real vector store gets replaced by a service that reports a configurable recall value, which sounds like cheating until we remember what we are measuring. We care about how the system behaves when recall drops, rather than about why it dropped.

CPU Path and Accelerator Path

The book runs on two paths, and every chapter marks which one applies. Our CPU path needs nothing beyond a laptop with eight gigabytes of memory and a container runtime. Everything in this chapter, along with the retrieval, model boundary, and agent chapters, runs happily on that path. Our accelerator path needs a machine with an NVIDIA GPU, and it applies only where the fault genuinely involves hardware. In Chapter 4 the distinction matters for the first time.

We keep both paths alive, which costs a little duplication and buys a great deal of reach. A reader without a GPU can still work through nine of the twelve chapters end to end. Our stand in inference service exposes exactly the same metric names as a real vLLM deployment would, so the probes never need rewriting. When a GPU does become available, swapping the image and adding a resource request is the whole migration.

Standing up Cluster

Creating Kind Cluster

We will build the cluster with kind, which runs Kubernetes nodes as containers on a single host. The three nodes give us one control plane and two workers, and we label the workers by pool so that scheduling stays predictable. We map two node ports through to the host, one for the gateway and one for Prometheus. Such mapping saves us from port forwarding during every experiment, which matters when a run lasts forty five minutes.

So, here's the cluster definition we need at **lab/kind-helpmate.yaml**:

```
kind: Cluster
apiVersion: kind.x-k8s.io/v1alpha4
name: helpmate
nodes:
  - role: control-plane
    kubeadmConfigPatches:
      - |
        kind: InitConfiguration
        nodeRegistration:
          kubeletExtraArgs:
            node-labels: "ingress-ready=true"
    extraPortMappings:
      - containerPort: 30080
        hostPort: 30080
        protocol: TCP
      - containerPort: 30090
        hostPort: 30090
        protocol: TCP
  - role: worker
    labels:
      helpmate.io/pool: serving
  - role: worker
    labels:
      helpmate.io/pool: data
```

Next, we create the cluster and confirm all three nodes register, like this:

```
kind create cluster --config lab/kind-helpmate.yaml
kubectl get nodes --show-labels -o wide
```

The three nodes appear within about ninety seconds, with the pool labels visible on the two workers.

```
NAME                       STATUS    ROLES           AGE    VERSION
helpmate-control-plane     Ready     control-plane   88s    v1.34.0
helpmate-worker            Ready     <none>          71s    v1.34.0
helpmate-worker2           Ready     <none>          71s    v1.34.0
```

Building and Loading HelpMate Image

A single image serves all four HelpMate roles, differentiated by an environment variable. Such a design keeps the lab small while preserving the four separate deployments we need for fault targeting. Our application exposes three endpoints, where **/healthz** reports readiness, **/ask** serves a request, and **/metrics** publishes everything in Prometheus text format. Every metric name matches what Chapter 2 declared, so no translation layer stands between the application and our probes.

Here's what we can now write in the application at **app/helpmate.py**:

```
"""One image, four roles. Each role exposes /healthz, /ask and
/metrics."""
from __future__ import annotations

import json
import os
import random
import time
import urllib.parse
from http.server import BaseHTTPRequestHandler, ThreadingHTTPServer
from urllib.request import urlopen

ROLE = os.environ.get("HELPMATE_ROLE", "gateway")
DOWNSTREAM = os.environ.get("HELPMATE_DOWNSTREAM", "")
RECALL_CENTRE = float(os.environ.get("HELPMATE_RECALL_CENTRE",
"0.81"))
REFUSAL_P = float(os.environ.get("HELPMATE_REFUSAL_P", "0.045"))

STATE = {
    "requests": 0,
    "refused": 0,
    "overridden": 0,
    "escalated": 0,
```

```
    "streams_complete": 0,
    "tool_calls": 0,
    "tool_calls_clean": 0,
    "ttft_buckets": {},
    "ttft_sum": 0.0,
    "recall_sum": 0.0,
    "tokens_sum": 0.0,
}
BUCKETS = [0.1, 0.25, 0.5, 0.75, 1.0, 1.5, 2.5, 5.0]
RNG = random.Random(int(os.environ.get("HELPMATE_SEED", "11")))


def observe_ttft(seconds: float) -> None:
    STATE["ttft_sum"] += seconds
    for edge in BUCKETS:
        if seconds <= edge:
            STATE["ttft_buckets"][edge] =
STATE["ttft_buckets"].get(edge, 0) + 1


def serve_one() -> dict:
    start = time.perf_counter()
    if DOWNSTREAM:
        try:
            urlopen(f"{DOWNSTREAM}/ask", timeout=2).read()
        except OSError:
            pass
    recall = min(1.0, max(0.0, RNG.gauss(RECALL_CENTRE, 0.11)))
    refused = RNG.random() < REFUSAL_P
    overridden = (not refused) and RNG.random() < (0.04 + 0.55 *
max(0.0, 0.80 - recall))
    planned = RNG.choice([0, 0, 1, 2, 3])
    clean = planned > 0 and RNG.random() > 0.02

    STATE["requests"] += 1
    STATE["refused"] += int(refused)
    STATE["overridden"] += int(overridden)
    STATE["escalated"] += int(overridden and RNG.random() < 0.28)
    STATE["streams_complete"] += int(RNG.random() > 0.004)
    STATE["tool_calls"] += int(planned > 0)
    STATE["tool_calls_clean"] += int(clean)
    STATE["recall_sum"] += recall
    STATE["tokens_sum"] += max(0.0, RNG.gauss(58.0, 6.5))
    observe_ttft(time.perf_counter() - start + RNG.lognormvariate(-
1.05, 0.34))
    return {"role": ROLE, "refused": refused, "recall_at_5":
```

```
round(recall, 4)}


def metrics() -> str:
    total = max(STATE["requests"], 1)
    lines = [
        "# TYPE helpmate_requests_total counter",
        f'helpmate_requests_total{{role="{ROLE}"}}
{STATE["requests"]}',
        "# TYPE helpmate_refused_total counter",
        f'helpmate_refused_total{{role="{ROLE}"}}
{STATE["refused"]}',
        "# TYPE helpmate_overridden_total counter",
        f'helpmate_overridden_total{{role="{ROLE}"}}
{STATE["overridden"]}',
        "# TYPE helpmate_escalated_total counter",
        f'helpmate_escalated_total{{role="{ROLE}"}}
{STATE["escalated"]}',
        "# TYPE helpmate_stream_complete_total counter",
        f'helpmate_stream_complete_total{{role="{ROLE}"}}
{STATE["streams_complete"]}',
        "# TYPE helpmate_tool_calls_total counter",
        f'helpmate_tool_calls_total{{role="{ROLE}"}}
{STATE["tool_calls"]}',
        "# TYPE helpmate_tool_calls_clean_total counter",
        f'helpmate_tool_calls_clean_total{{role="{ROLE}"}}
{STATE["tool_calls_clean"]}',
        "# TYPE helpmate_recall_at_5 gauge",
        f'helpmate_recall_at_5{{role="{ROLE}"}}
{STATE["recall_sum"] / total:.4f}',
        "# TYPE helpmate_tokens_per_second gauge",
        f'helpmate_tokens_per_second{{role="{ROLE}"}}
{STATE["tokens_sum"] / total:.2f}',
        "# TYPE helpmate_ttft_seconds histogram",
    ]
    for edge in BUCKETS:
        seen = STATE["ttft_buckets"].get(edge, 0)

lines.append(f'helpmate_ttft_seconds_bucket{{role="{ROLE}",le="{edg
e}"}} {seen}')

lines.append(f'helpmate_ttft_seconds_bucket{{role="{ROLE}",le="+Inf
"}} {STATE["requests"]}')
    lines.append(f'helpmate_ttft_seconds_sum{{role="{ROLE}"}}
{STATE["ttft_sum"]:.4f}')
    lines.append(f'helpmate_ttft_seconds_count{{role="{ROLE}"}}
```

```
{STATE["requests"]}')
    return "\n".join(lines) + "\n"


class Handler(BaseHTTPRequestHandler):
    def log_message(self, *args) -> None:
        return

    def do_GET(self) -> None:
        if self.path.startswith("/healthz"):
            body, ctype = json.dumps({"role": ROLE, "ok": True}),
"application/json"
        elif self.path.startswith("/metrics"):
            body, ctype = metrics(), "text/plain; version=0.0.4"
        elif self.path.startswith("/ask"):
            body, ctype = json.dumps(serve_one()),
"application/json"
        else:
            self.send_error(404)
            return
        payload = body.encode()
        self.send_response(200)
        self.send_header("Content-Type", ctype)
        self.send_header("Content-Length", str(len(payload)))
        self.end_headers()
        self.wfile.write(payload)


if __name__ == "__main__":
    port = int(os.environ.get("HELPMATE_PORT", "8080"))
    print(f"helpmate role={ROLE} listening on {port}", flush=True)
    ThreadingHTTPServer(("0.0.0.0", port), Handler).serve_forever()
```

The histogram deserves careful attention, since it trips up more people than any other part of the Prometheus format. Our **observe_ttft** helper increments every bucket whose edge sits above the observed value, which produces the cumulative counts Prometheus expects. Anything else, such as per bucket counts, would make **histogram_quantile** return nonsense without ever raising an error. We also emit the **_sum** and **_count** series, because omitting them breaks several standard functions silently.

The build and the load into the cluster go like this:

```
cat > Dockerfile <<'DOCKER'
FROM python:3.12-slim
WORKDIR /srv
COPY app/helpmate.py /srv/helpmate.py
```

```
ENV HELPMATE_PORT=8080
EXPOSE 8080
ENTRYPOINT ["python3", "/srv/helpmate.py"]
DOCKER

docker build -t helpmate:1.0 .
kind load docker-image helpmate:1.0 --name helpmate
```

Here, a quick verification is needed and very useful too. The image should appear on every node rather than on one, since a pod scheduled onto a worker without it will sit in ImagePullBackOff and look like a networking fault. The loading of the image directly into kind also means no registry sits anywhere in our path, so a registry outage can never be mistaken for something we injected.

Deploying HelpMate and Prometheus

Our deployment manifest creates four deployments and four services inside the **`helpmate-staging`** namespace. Each pod carries two labels that matter later, where **`app`** identifies the fault target and **`helpmate.io/layer`** identifies the taxonomy layer we fixed at the outset. Both labels flow into Prometheus through relabelling, which lets us slice any signal by layer during an experiment. Our gateway chains to the agent, the agent chains to the retriever, and that chain gives us a real propagation path to break.

Having settled that, here's how the application and observability manifests get applied:

```
kubectl apply -f lab/helpmate.yaml
kubectl apply -f lab/prometheus.yaml
kubectl -n helpmate-staging rollout status deploy/helpmate-gateway
--timeout=120s
curl -s localhost:30080/healthz
```

After this, a single JSON line like **`{"role": "gateway", "ok": true}`** confirms that the gateway is serving through the mapped node port.

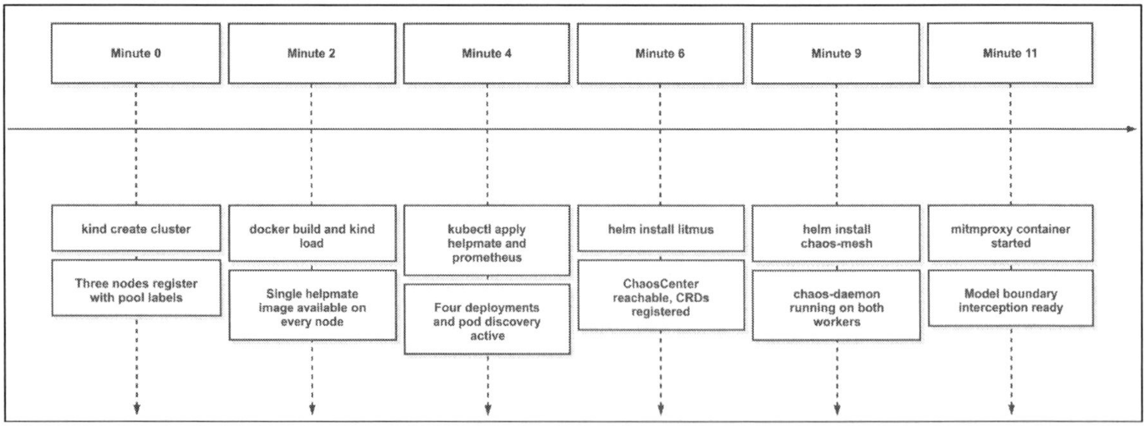

Installing Three Tools

LitmusChaos as Orchestration Spine

Our orchestration load for the whole book falls on LitmusChaos. Every experiment we schedule becomes a **ChaosEngine** resource, which means our experiments live in Git alongside the application manifests. The resilience probes matter even more than the fault library, since a probe is how our Chapter 2 envelopes become machine checkable during a run. A cluster scoped installation was deprecated at the 3.9.0 release, so namespaced installation is the only supported mode now.

Next comes the chart repository and the ChaosCenter install, which run like this:

```
helm repo add litmuschaos https://litmuschaos.github.io/litmus-
helm/
helm repo update
kubectl create namespace litmus

helm install chaos litmuschaos/litmus \
  --namespace litmus \
  --version 3.29.1 \
  --set portal.frontend.service.type=NodePort
```

A short wait brings every component to running, which we confirm before going further.

```
kubectl -n litmus get pods
```

```
NAME                                    READY    STATUS     RESTARTS
AGE
chaos-litmus-auth-server-6b47d9c-4kx2t  1/1      Running    0
2m14s
chaos-litmus-frontend-79f5c8d5c-nzq7p   1/1      Running    0
2m14s
chaos-litmus-server-5d9b7c4f8-t8xvw     1/1      Running    0
2m14s
chaos-mongodb-0                         1/1      Running    0
2m14s
```

A prerequisite catches people out during installation. The ChaosCenter component needs a persistent volume for its MongoDB instance, and kind provides a default local path provisioner that satisfies this. The documented production recommendation is twenty gigabytes, though one gigabyte serves us perfectly well in the lab. Should the MongoDB pod sit in pending, a missing storage class is almost always the reason.

Chaos Mesh for Fault Depth

The faults Litmus cannot reach fall to Chaos Mesh. We need filesystem level injection through **IOChaos** for our model artifact work, while **TimeChaos** and **KernelChaos** have no equivalent anywhere in the Litmus library. The fine grained **NetworkChaos** resource gives us per direction latency and loss, which we need when a streaming response degrades in only one direction. Both tools run together with no special handling, since their controllers watch different custom resources and never contend.

An installation detail deserves attention, because getting it wrong produces a **chaos-daemon** that starts and then does nothing useful. The tool needs the container runtime socket, and the path differs by runtime. Our kind cluster uses containerd, so the socket sits at **/run/containerd/containerd.sock** rather than at the Docker path most examples show. We also disable leader election, since three controller replicas on a two worker lab wastes memory for no benefit.

With that in place, here's how Chaos Mesh gets installed against the containerd socket:

```
helm repo add chaos-mesh https://charts.chaos-mesh.org
helm repo update
kubectl create namespace chaos-mesh

helm install chaos-mesh chaos-mesh/chaos-mesh \
  --namespace chaos-mesh \
  --version 2.8.3 \
  --set chaosDaemon.runtime=containerd \
  --set chaosDaemon.socketPath=/run/containerd/containerd.sock \
  --set controllerManager.leaderElection.enabled=false \
  --set dashboard.securityMode=false
```

We verify one controller, one daemon per worker, and the dashboard.

```
kubectl get pods -n chaos-mesh -l app.kubernetes.io/instance=chaos-
mesh
```

```
NAME                                       READY    STATUS
RESTARTS    AGE
chaos-controller-manager-676d8567c7-ndr5j  1/1      Running    0
96s
chaos-daemon-6155b                         1/1      Running    0
96s
chaos-daemon-p2xkq                         1/1      Running    0
96s
chaos-dashboard-b9dbc6b68-hln25            1/1      Running    0
96s
```

'mitmproxy' at Model Boundary

Our third tool solves a problem neither Kubernetes tool can touch. A fault on response content, such as a truncated completion or a tool call argument that violates its schema, lives above the network layer entirely. The Chaos Mesh controller can delay a packet, and it cannot rewrite the JSON inside one. We therefore place mitmproxy between the agent and the inference service, where a Python addon can mutate any field in a response before it reaches the caller.

The installation stays light, since mitmproxy runs as an ordinary container with no cluster privileges. The addon set gets developed properly once we reach the model boundary, so for now we only confirm the interception path works. Our agent deployment gains an environment variable pointing at the proxy, and the proxy forwards to the inference service unchanged. A first run in passthrough mode proves the plumbing without altering a single byte.

Why Three and Not Thirty?

Many capable alternatives exist, and choosing three is a deliberate constraint rather than a judgement about quality. The ChaosBlade project covers host, container, and JVM faults with a pleasant command line. Krkn brings node and zone level scenarios along with an evolutionary approach to scenario refinement, and it entered the CNCF Sandbox in January 2026. The Chaos Toolkit offers a provider agnostic experiment format. Any of them would serve a team well, and adding all of them would serve nobody.

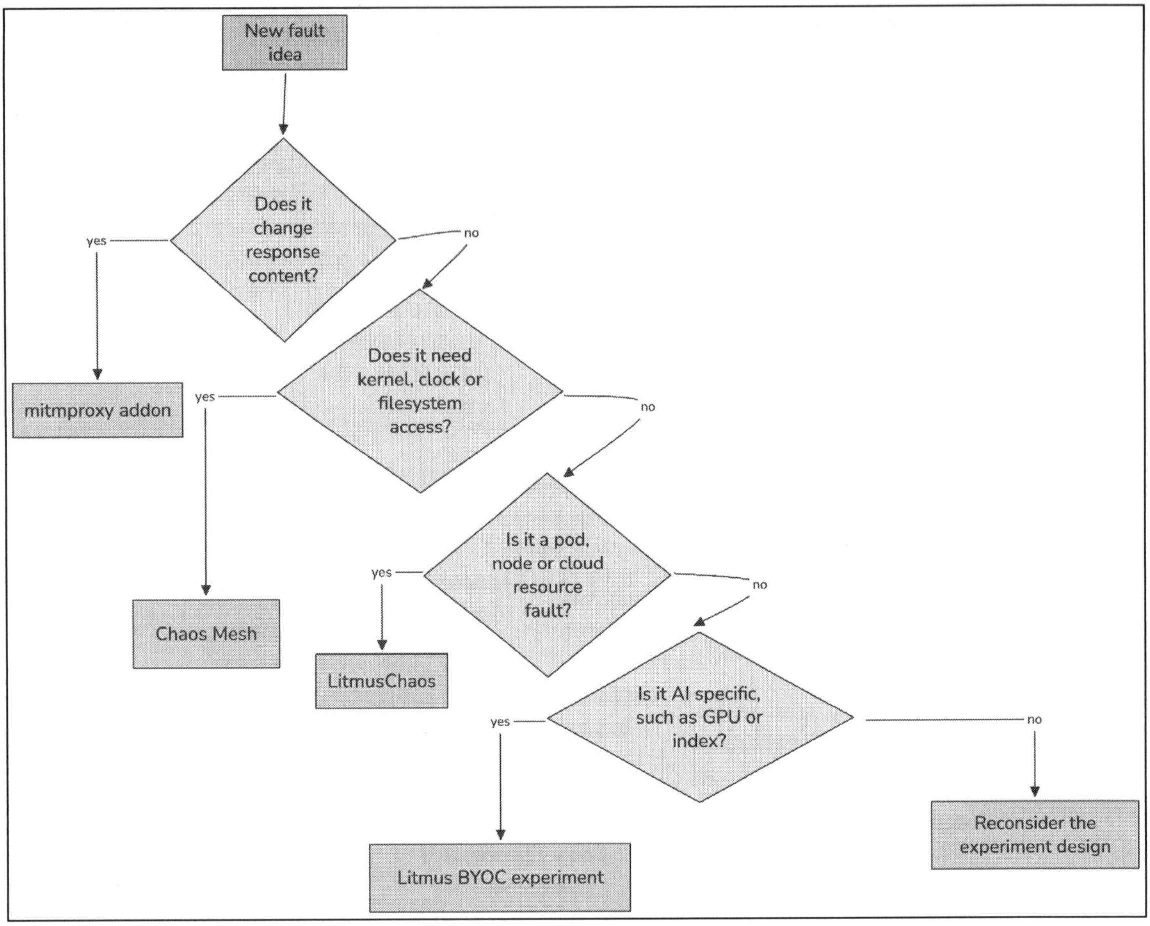

Every fault in this book routes through that decision cleanly, which is the practical test of whether three tools suffice. Our ongoing cost matters more than our installation cost, because each tool carries version upgrades, custom resource churn, and one more thing to debug at midnight. A team fluent in three tools outperforms a team passingly familiar with eight. Should a genuine gap appear later, adding a fourth tool deliberately beats installing six speculatively today.

Connecting Steady State to Live Telemetry

Reducing Signals from Prometheus

Our reduction step now needs a second implementation. The file based version from Chapter 2 stays exactly as written, since we still use captures for offline analysis. Alongside it we add a Prometheus backed version producing an identical dictionary, which means every downstream piece keeps working untouched. Such symmetry is the payoff for having separated envelope arithmetic from data collection in the first place.

Our next task is the Prometheus reduction at **probes/reduce_prom.py**, and here's what it holds:

```
"""Same signal reduction as reduce.py, sourced from Prometheus
instead of a file."""
from __future__ import annotations

import json
import urllib.parse
import urllib.request
from typing import Any

WINDOW = "5m"

QUERIES = {
    "ttft_p99_ms": (
        "histogram_quantile(0.99, "
        "sum by (le) (rate(helpmate_ttft_seconds_bucket[%s]))) *
1000" % WINDOW
    ),
    "tokens_per_second": "avg(helpmate_tokens_per_second)",
    "recall_at_5": "avg(helpmate_recall_at_5)",
    "refusal_rate": (
        "sum(rate(helpmate_refused_total[%s])) "
        "/ sum(rate(helpmate_requests_total[%s]))" % (WINDOW,
WINDOW)
    ),
    "override_rate": (
        "sum(rate(helpmate_overridden_total[%s])) "
        "/ clamp_min(sum(rate(helpmate_requests_total[%s])) "
        "- sum(rate(helpmate_refused_total[%s])), 0.001)" %
(WINDOW, WINDOW, WINDOW)
    ),
    "escalation_rate": (
        "sum(rate(helpmate_escalated_total[%s])) "
        "/ sum(rate(helpmate_requests_total[%s]))" % (WINDOW,
WINDOW)
    ),
    "stream_completion_rate": (
        "sum(rate(helpmate_stream_complete_total[%s])) "
        "/ sum(rate(helpmate_requests_total[%s]))" % (WINDOW,
WINDOW)
    ),
    "tool_call_success": (
        "sum(rate(helpmate_tool_calls_clean_total[%s])) "
```

```
        "/ clamp_min(sum(rate(helpmate_tool_calls_total[%s])),
0.001)" % (WINDOW, WINDOW)
    ),
}


def query_one(endpoint: str, expression: str, timeout: float = 5.0)
-> float:
    url = f"{endpoint}/api/v1/query?" +
urllib.parse.urlencode({"query": expression})
    with urllib.request.urlopen(url, timeout=timeout) as response:
        payload: dict[str, Any] = json.loads(response.read())
    if payload.get("status") != "success":
        raise RuntimeError(f"prometheus rejected the query:
{expression}")
    result = payload["data"]["result"]
    if not result:
        raise RuntimeError(f"prometheus returned no series for:
{expression}")
    return float(result[0]["value"][1])


def reduce_signals_from_prometheus(endpoint: str) -> dict[str,
float]:
    values = {}
    for name, expression in QUERIES.items():
        values[name] = round(query_one(endpoint, expression), 4)
    return values
```

A pair of details in those queries repays a second look. Our override rate divides by served requests rather than by all requests, matching the denominator decision from Chapter 2, and **`clamp_min`** protects us from division by zero during quiet periods. An error raised on an empty result matters just as much, since a silently missing series would otherwise reduce to zero and pass every floor check. A probe that cannot distinguish healthy from absent is worse than no probe at all.

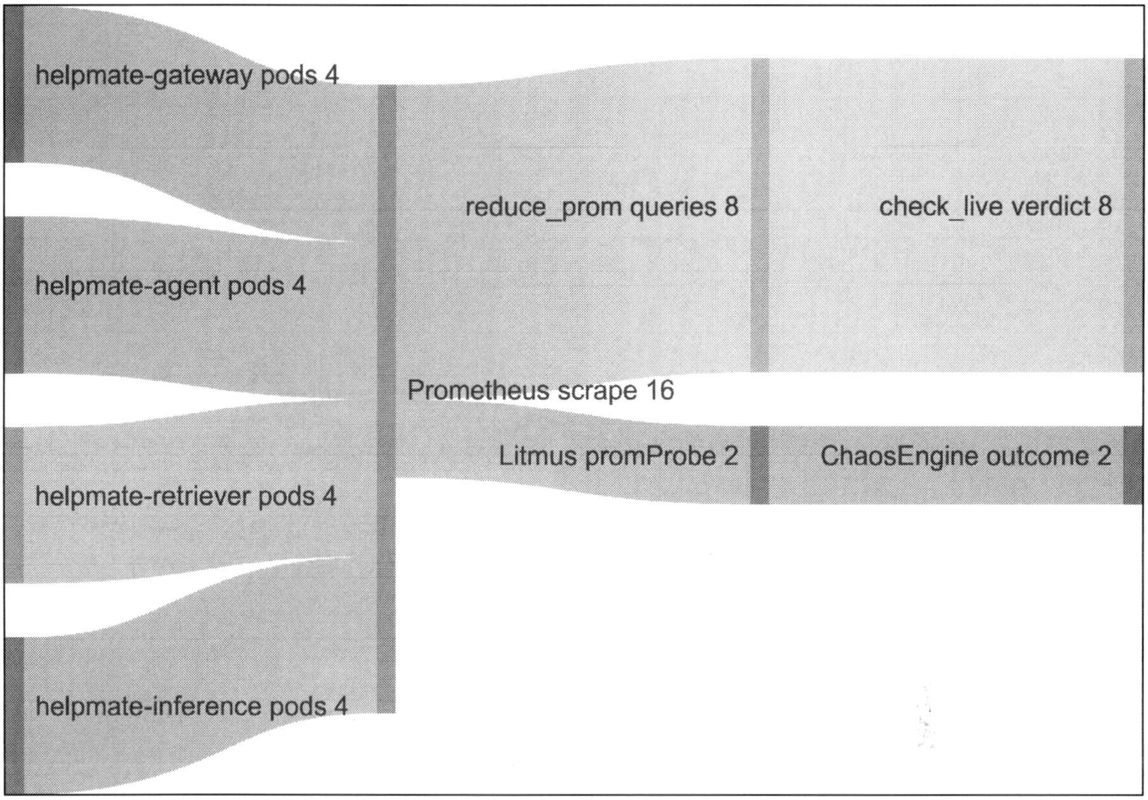

So, here's the live checker at **probes/check_live.py** and the command that runs it:

```
"""Evaluate the live cluster against the declared envelopes."""
from __future__ import annotations

import argparse
from pathlib import Path

from probes.check import report
from probes.envelope import load_envelopes
from probes.reduce_prom import reduce_signals_from_prometheus


def main() -> None:
    parser = argparse.ArgumentParser(description="Check live
signals against envelopes")
    parser.add_argument("--endpoint",
default="http://localhost:30090")
    parser.add_argument("--signals",
default="signals/helpmate.yaml")
    args = parser.parse_args()
```

```
    values = reduce_signals_from_prometheus(args.endpoint)
    envelopes = load_envelopes(Path(args.signals))
    breached = report(values, envelopes)
    print("-" * 66)
    print(f"live sample, {len(breached)} breach(es)")
    if breached:
        print("breached:", ", ".join(breached))
    raise SystemExit(1 if breached else 0)


if __name__ == "__main__":
    main()
```

A few minutes of traffic first gives Prometheus something to rate over.

```
RPS=8 SECONDS_TO_RUN=300 bash lab/load.sh &
sleep 300
python3 -m probes.check_live --endpoint http://localhost:30090
```

Our live sample reports the same eight signals the capture file produced, now sourced from the cluster.

```
signal                         value     floor   ceiling  status
------------------------------------------------------------------
escalation_rate               0.0181         -      0.06  inside
override_rate                 0.0503         -     0.085  inside
recall_at_5                   0.8011     0.733         -  inside
refusal_rate                  0.0462      0.01    0.0925  inside
stream_completion_rate        0.9968    0.9825         -  inside
tokens_per_second              58.02     51.23         -  inside
tool_call_success             0.9724    0.9304         -  inside
ttft_p99_ms                    661.4         -     833.9  inside
------------------------------------------------------------------
live sample, 0 breach(es)
```

Guarding against Probe Drift

A new failure mode appears the moment thresholds exist in two places. Our envelopes live in **signals/helpmate.yaml**, while Litmus probe comparators live inside each **ChaosEngine**. Somebody widens an envelope after a noisy week, forgets the probe, and every subsequent experiment silently tests against the old number. No error appears, no warning fires, and the results quietly stop meaning what the file says they mean.

For now, we can add a drift guard at **probes/sync_check.py** like this:

```
"""Fail when a probe threshold drifts away from the committed
envelope."""
from __future__ import annotations

import argparse
from pathlib import Path

import yaml

from probes.envelope import load_envelopes

BINDINGS = {
    "recall-stays-above-floor": ("recall_at_5", "floor"),
    "ttft-stays-below-ceiling": ("ttft_p99_ms", "ceiling"),
    "override-stays-below-ceiling": ("override_rate", "ceiling"),
}


def collect_probes(engine: dict) -> list[dict]:
    found = []
    for experiment in engine["spec"].get("experiments", []):
        found.extend(experiment["spec"].get("probe", []))
    return found


def main() -> None:
    parser = argparse.ArgumentParser(description="Compare probes
against signals")
    parser.add_argument("engine")
    parser.add_argument("--signals",
default="signals/helpmate.yaml")
    args = parser.parse_args()

    engine =
yaml.safe_load(Path(args.engine).read_text(encoding="utf-8"))
    envelopes = load_envelopes(Path(args.signals))
    problems = []
    checked = 0

    for probe in collect_probes(engine):
        binding = BINDINGS.get(probe["name"])
        if binding is None:
            continue
        signal, bound = binding
        declared = getattr(envelopes[signal], bound)
```

```
        asserted =
float(probe["promProbe/inputs"]["comparator"]["value"])
        checked += 1
        if declared is None or abs(declared - asserted) > 1e-9:
            problems.append(
                f"probe '{probe['name']}' asserts {asserted}, "
                f"but {signal} {bound} is {declared}"
            )

    for problem in problems:
        print(f"drift: {problem}")
    if problems:
        raise SystemExit(1)
    print(f"in sync: {checked} probe threshold(s) match
signals/helpmate.yaml")


if __name__ == "__main__":
    main()
```

Our guard joins the validator from Chapter 2 inside continuous integration, so neither file can move without the other. A run against a deliberately tampered copy confirms the check has teeth.

```
sed 's/value: "833.9"/value: "1200.0"/' \
  experiments/exp-002-gateway-pod-delete.yaml > /tmp/drifted.yaml
python3 -m probes.sync_check /tmp/drifted.yaml
```

```
drift: probe 'ttft-stays-below-ceiling' asserts 1200.0, but
ttft_p99_ms ceiling is 833.9
```

First End-to-End Experiment

Pod Delete on Idle Cluster

Our first experiment deletes half the gateway replicas over sixty seconds. None of that is interesting on its own, and the point is to prove the whole chain works before we attempt anything subtle. We attach three probes to the engine, where two query Prometheus continuously and one checks gateway health at the end. Both Prometheus thresholds come straight from our committed envelopes, which the drift guard now enforces.

Here's the engine we need at **`experiments/exp-002-gateway-pod-delete.yaml`**:

```yaml
apiVersion: litmuschaos.io/v1alpha1
kind: ChaosEngine
metadata:
  name: exp-002-gateway-pod-delete
  namespace: helpmate-staging
spec:
  engineState: active
  annotationCheck: "false"
  chaosServiceAccount: litmus-admin
  jobCleanUpPolicy: retain
  appinfo:
    appns: helpmate-staging
    applabel: app=helpmate-gateway
    appkind: deployment
  experiments:
    - name: pod-delete
      spec:
        components:
          env:
            - name: TOTAL_CHAOS_DURATION
              value: "60"
            - name: CHAOS_INTERVAL
              value: "20"
            - name: PODS_AFFECTED_PERC
              value: "50"
            - name: FORCE
              value: "false"
        probe:
          - name: recall-stays-above-floor
            type: promProbe
            mode: Continuous
            runProperties:
              probeTimeout: 5s
              interval: 10s
              retry: 2
            promProbe/inputs:
              endpoint: http://prometheus.observability.svc:9090
              query: avg(helpmate_recall_at_5)
              comparator:
                criteria: ">="
                value: "0.733"
          - name: ttft-stays-below-ceiling
            type: promProbe
            mode: Continuous
            runProperties:
```

```
          probeTimeout: 5s
          interval: 10s
          retry: 2
        promProbe/inputs:
          endpoint: http://prometheus.observability.svc:9090
          query: |
            histogram_quantile(0.99,
              sum by (le)
(rate(helpmate_ttft_seconds_bucket[2m]))) * 1000
          comparator:
            criteria: "<="
            value: "833.9"
      - name: gateway-answers-after-chaos
        type: httpProbe
        mode: EOT
        runProperties:
          probeTimeout: 5s
          interval: 5s
          retry: 3
        httpProbe/inputs:
          url: http://helpmate-gateway.helpmate-
staging.svc:8080/healthz
          insecureSkipVerify: false
          method:
            get:
              criteria: ==
              responseCode: "200"
```

A run against an idle cluster produces the result we expect, and the boredom is the point.

```
python3 -m probes.sync_check experiments/exp-002-gateway-pod-
delete.yaml
kubectl apply -f experiments/exp-002-gateway-pod-delete.yaml
kubectl -n helpmate-staging get chaosresult \
  exp-002-gateway-pod-delete-pod-delete -o
jsonpath='{.status.experimentStatus.verdict}'
```

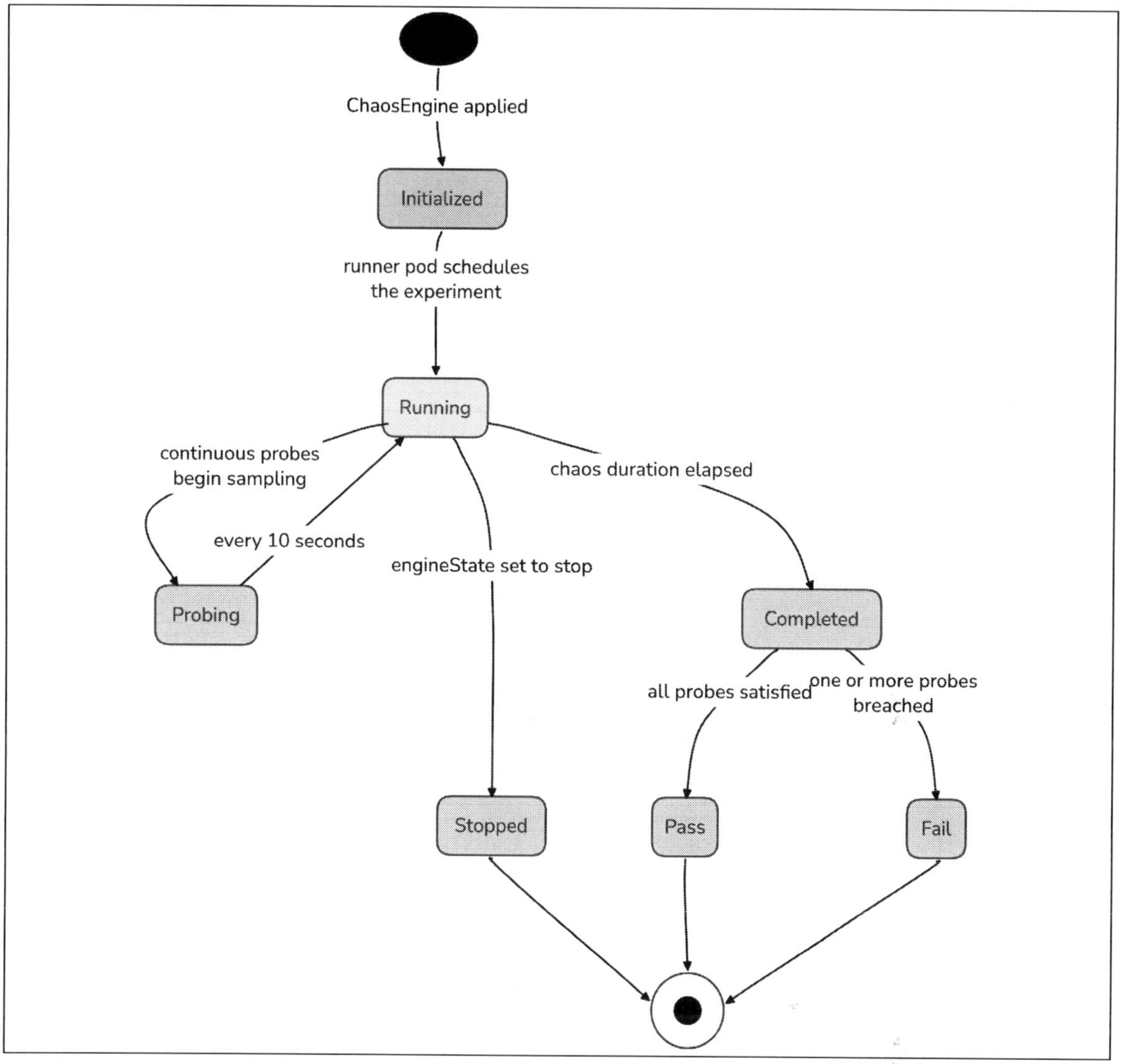

Deletion under Load

The same experiment with the load generator running changes the result entirely. Our idle run had no in flight requests to lose, so a graceful eviction cost nothing. Under eight requests per second, each deleted pod carries live connections that terminate mid response. The stream completion rate dips for roughly fifteen seconds, and time to first token rises while the replacement warms up.

Neither run breaches an envelope, which surprises people who expected a dramatic first experiment. Our finding is nonetheless useful, because we now know the graceful eviction path holds under this load and we know the recovery shape. In Chapter 4 we raise the pressure considerably by moving down to the accelerator layer, where the faults have no graceful path at all.

Recording Findings

Every chapter from here forward closes with the same five columns. Our verdict comes from the closed vocabulary fixed at the start of the book, and the finding states what the run actually taught us rather than what we hoped it would.

Fault	Tool	Signal watched	Verdict	Finding
Pod delete, 50 percent, idle cluster	Litmus	stream_completion_rate, ttft_p99_ms	Absorbed	Baseline proof the chain works end to end, no signal moved
Pod delete, 50 percent, 8 req/s	Litmus	stream_completion_rate, ttft_p99_ms	Absorbed	Completion dipped to 0.991 for 15s, recovered inside the envelope
Pod delete with grace period set to 1s	Litmus	stream_completion_rate	Degraded	Completion fell to 0.94, breaching the 0.9825 floor and alerting correctly
Prometheus scrape target misconfigured	manual	all eight signals	Silent	Probes reported success against absent series until we added the empty result guard

That final row came from our own mistake rather than from a planned experiment. Our first relabelling configuration rewrote the scrape address incorrectly, so Prometheus returned no series and the reduction happily produced zeros. Every floor check passed, since zero compared against a ceiling looks healthy. The empty result guard inside **`query_one`** was the direct consequence, and the row stays in the table as a reminder.

Summary

We turned an empty machine into a working chaos laboratory. Our three node kind cluster now runs four HelpMate deployments from a single image, alongside Prometheus with pod discovery and layer aware relabelling. Our orchestration runs through LitmusChaos, Chaos Mesh reaches the kernel and filesystem faults Litmus cannot, and mitmproxy waits at the model boundary for the content faults neither Kubernetes tool can produce. A routing decision now tells us which tool owns any new fault idea.

Our steady state work from Chapter 2 connected to that cluster without changing a line of envelope arithmetic. The Prometheus reduction produces the same dictionary the capture file produced, and a drift guard refuses to let probe thresholds diverge from the committed envelopes.

A pair of pod delete runs proved the chain works end to end, while a fourth row in our findings table recorded a silent failure we caused ourselves. In Chapter 4 we move down to the accelerator layer, where graceful degradation stops being available.

CHAPTER 4

ACCELERATOR AND COMPUTE CHAOS

In Chapter 3 we ended with two pod deletes that both landed on absorbed. The graceful eviction held, the replacement warmed up, and nothing moved outside its envelope. Such a result is reassuring and slightly misleading, because Kubernetes was designed to make exactly that fault survivable. We now move down to the layer where no orchestrator can help us, since a throttled accelerator cannot be rescheduled away from its own thermal budget.

Across this chapter, we will throttle compute deliberately on both the accelerator path and the CPU path, then drain a node under live traffic. Our comparison machinery arrives here as well, where a small module turns a before and after pair into one of our four verdicts without human judgement. We will prove those rules against synthetic cases before trusting them on real runs. By the close, four experiments will have produced four different verdicts, and we will have recorded exactly what we chose not to attempt.

What is Accelerator Layer?

Faults with No Graceful Path

Every fault in Chapter 3 had an escape route built into the platform. A deleted pod gets replaced, a full queue sheds load, and a slow node stops receiving work. No such route exists once compute itself starves. When a GPU enforces a lower power limit, the clocks drop and every request served by that device becomes slower. A reschedule helps only when another device has headroom, which in a saturated fleet is precisely the situation that never holds. The consequences are twofold, and both shape how we design experiments here. Our blast radius cannot be reduced by touching fewer pods, since the fault lives below the pod boundary and affects everything sharing the device. The recovery also behaves differently, because restoring a power limit returns performance immediately while a restarted pod needs to warm its cache. We therefore treat the accelerator layer as the one place where the injection must carry its own restore path rather than relying on Kubernetes to clean up.

These faults also arrive gradually in production rather than all at once. A thermal throttle ramps as ambient temperature climbs through an afternoon. The power cap tightens as a rack approaches its budget. Neither event produces a moment where something clearly broke, which is exactly the profile our envelopes were built to catch. A signal drifting steadily toward its floor across four hours looks like nothing at all on a dashboard scaled to the previous week.

Paths and their Faults

In the previous chapter, we introduced the accelerator path and the CPU path without needing the distinction. Here the distinction becomes real for the first time. Our accelerator path requires a machine with an NVIDIA device, and it reaches the genuine hardware behaviour where clocks fall and power draw drops. A reader on the CPU path uses a headroom endpoint built into HelpMate, which reproduces the observable effect on our signals without reproducing the cause.

That substitution is defensible for one specific reason. Our experiments measure how the system responds to reduced compute, rather than measuring why compute reduced. A throttled GPU and a software headroom cut both push **tokens_per_second** down and **ttft_p99_ms** up, and both leave retrieval quality untouched. Every probe, every envelope, and every verdict behaves identically across the two paths. A team that later gains real hardware swaps the injection mechanism and changes nothing else. A caveat belongs alongside that claim. Our software substitute cannot reproduce second order hardware effects, such as memory bandwidth contention or the way clock throttling interacts with a large batch. Such effects matter, and they only appear on real devices. We therefore treat CPU path results as directionally correct rather than as final numbers, and we re-run the same experiments on hardware before trusting any threshold derived from them.

Throttling Compute on Purpose

Accelerator Path with 'nvidia-smi'

Our accelerator injection lowers the enforced power limit on one device, holds it, then restores the original value. The script rests on three properties more than anything else. The default limit gets read from the device rather than hardcoded, so the restore path cannot write a wrong value. A trap installs the restore before the throttle is applied, which means an interrupted run still recovers. We enable persistence mode first, since a driver unload would otherwise discard our setting unpredictably.

So, here's what you need to write in that injection script at **experiments/accelerator/gpu-power-limit.sh**:

```
#!/usr/bin/env bash
# Lower the enforced power limit on one GPU, hold it, then restore
the default.
set -euo pipefail

GPU_INDEX="${GPU_INDEX:-0}"
TARGET_WATTS="${TARGET_WATTS:-150}"
HOLD_SECONDS="${HOLD_SECONDS:-300}"

report() {
  nvidia-smi --id="${GPU_INDEX}" \
    --query-
gpu=index,power.draw,power.limit,power.default_limit,clocks.sm \
    --format=csv,noheader
}

DEFAULT_WATTS="$(nvidia-smi --id="${GPU_INDEX}" \
  --query-gpu=power.default_limit --format=csv,noheader,nounits |
tr -d ' ')"
```

```
echo "$(date -Is) gpu ${GPU_INDEX} default limit is
${DEFAULT_WATTS} W"
echo "$(date -Is) before: $(report)"

restore() {
  echo "$(date -Is) restoring gpu ${GPU_INDEX} to ${DEFAULT_WATTS}
W"
  nvidia-smi --id="${GPU_INDEX}" --power-limit="${DEFAULT_WATTS}"
|| true
  echo "$(date -Is) after: $(report)"
}
trap restore EXIT INT TERM

nvidia-smi --id="${GPU_INDEX}" --persistence-mode=1
nvidia-smi --id="${GPU_INDEX}" --power-limit="${TARGET_WATTS}"
echo "$(date -Is) throttled: $(report)"

sleep "${HOLD_SECONDS}"
```

The trap on **`TERM`** alongside **`EXIT`** and **`INT`** deserves emphasis, since that single word separates a safe experiment from a permanently throttled device. When we delete the Job, Kubernetes sends **`SIGTERM`** and waits for the grace period. Without the trap, the container dies with the power limit still applied and nobody notices until somebody wonders why inference got slow last Tuesday. Our grace period is set to thirty seconds, which leaves ample room for two **`nvidia-smi`** calls.

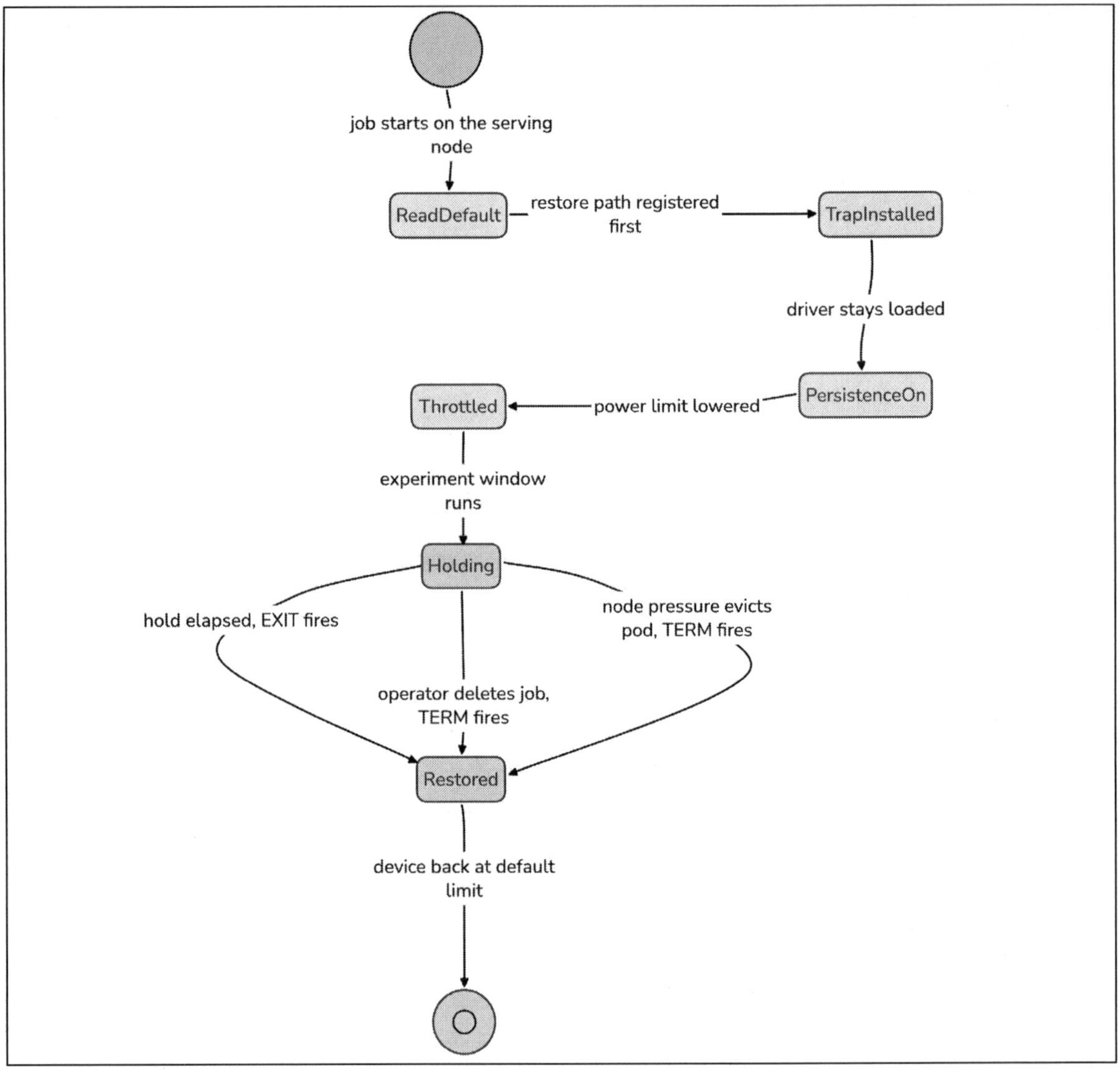

The next step is to run the throttle as a privileged Job pinned to the serving pool as below:

```
kubectl -n helpmate-staging create configmap accelerator-scripts \
  --from-file=experiments/accelerator/gpu-power-limit.sh
kubectl apply -f experiments/accelerator/throttle-job.yaml
kubectl -n helpmate-staging logs -f job/gpu-power-limit
```

The log shows the device settling at the lower limit, with clocks falling accordingly.

```
2026-08-12T09:14:02+00:00 gpu 0 default limit is 300 W
2026-08-12T09:14:02+00:00 before: 0, 271.44 W, 300.00 W, 300.00 W,
1980 MHz
```

```
2026-08-12T09:14:03+00:00 throttled: 0, 148.90 W, 150.00 W, 300.00
W, 1155 MHz
```

CPU Path with Headroom Endpoint

Our software substitute adds one administrative endpoint to the HelpMate application from Chapter 3. A single headroom ratio scales throughput down and latency up, which reproduces the observable shape of a throttled device. We expose the ratio as its own gauge, because an experiment that cannot report how hard it pushed is difficult to reproduce later.

The headroom control then extends **`app/helpmate.py`** like this:

```
# Compute headroom, expressed as a fraction of nominal. The
accelerator path
# lowers this with nvidia-smi; the CPU path lowers it through
/admin/throttle.
HEADROOM = {"value": 1.0}


def serve_one() -> dict:
    ...
    headroom = max(0.05, HEADROOM["value"])
    STATE["tokens_sum"] += max(0.0, RNG.gauss(58.0, 6.5)) *
headroom
    latency = RNG.lognormvariate(-1.05, 0.34) / headroom
    observe_ttft(time.perf_counter() - start + latency)
    return {"role": ROLE, "refused": refused, "recall_at_5":
round(recall, 4)}
```

Our request handler gains a matching branch, and the metrics endpoint gains one gauge.

```
        elif self.path.startswith("/admin/throttle"):
            query = urllib.parse.urlparse(self.path).query
            asked = urllib.parse.parse_qs(query).get("headroom",
["1.0"])[0]
            HEADROOM["value"] = min(1.0, max(0.05, float(asked)))
            body = json.dumps({"headroom": HEADROOM["value"]})
            ctype = "application/json"

        "# TYPE helpmate_compute_headroom_ratio gauge",
        f'helpmate_compute_headroom_ratio{{role="{ROLE}"}}
{HEADROOM["value"]:.4f}',
```

The throttle takes one request against the inference service.

```
kubectl -n helpmate-staging port-forward svc/helpmate-inference
8080:8080 &
curl -s "localhost:8080/admin/throttle?headroom=0.87"
```

```
{"headroom": 0.87}
```

Before vs. After

Assigning Verdict Mechanically

Our four words have been applied by hand so far, which will not survive a growing programme. Any two engineers looking at identical numbers should reach identical verdicts, and the only way to guarantee that is to encode the rules. The decision takes three inputs, namely which signals breached, which layers those signals belong to, and whether the system reported the breach itself.

The third input takes the most care to define. A breach counts as reported when it lands in a layer whose failures surface through ordinary errors and alerts, or when the system raises its own distress signals. The accelerator, serving, and artifact breaches fall into the first group, since a slow response and a failed stream both produce visible symptoms. A rise in refusals or escalations falls into the second group, because both represent the system openly admitting it cannot cope.

Here's what the verdict rules look like at **probes/verdict.py**:

```
"""Assign one of the four verdicts by comparing a baseline against
an injection."""
from __future__ import annotations

from dataclasses import dataclass, field

from probes.envelope import Envelope

# Layers whose breach the system itself would surface through an
error or alert.
REPORTING_LAYERS = {"accelerator", "serving", "artifact"}
# Signals that constitute the system admitting distress in its own
output.
DISTRESS_SIGNALS = {"refusal_rate", "escalation_rate"}


@dataclass
class Comparison:
    injection_layer: str
    breached: list[str] = field(default_factory=list)
```

```
    breached_layers: set[str] = field(default_factory=set)
    reported: bool = False

    @property
    def verdict(self) -> str:
        if not self.breached:
            return "absorbed"
        if not self.reported:
            return "silent"
        if self.breached_layers - {self.injection_layer}:
            return "cascaded"
        return "degraded"


def compare(
    baseline: dict[str, float],
    injection: dict[str, float],
    envelopes: dict[str, Envelope],
    injection_layer: str,
) -> Comparison:
    result = Comparison(injection_layer=injection_layer)
    for name, value in injection.items():
        env = envelopes.get(name)
        if env is None or env.holds(value):
            continue
        result.breached.append(name)
        result.breached_layers.add(env.layer)
        if env.layer in REPORTING_LAYERS or name in
DISTRESS_SIGNALS:
            result.reported = True
    result.breached.sort()
    return result


def deltas(
    baseline: dict[str, float], injection: dict[str, float]
) -> dict[str, float]:
    shared = set(baseline) & set(injection)
    return {name: round(injection[name] - baseline[name], 4) for
name in sorted(shared)}
```

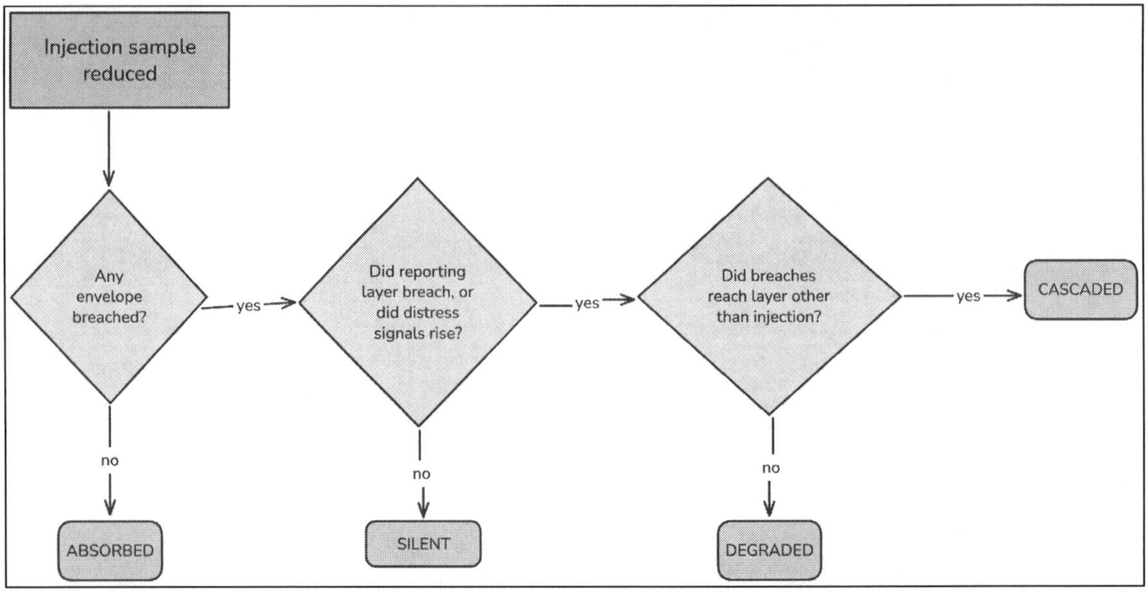

The word silent deliberately outranks cascaded in that ordering, and the priority is not arbitrary. A fault spreading across three layers while every alert stays quiet is worse than the same spread with alarms firing, since nobody will ever hear about the first case. Our vocabulary should reward visibility rather than confine itself to describing scope. A reader tempted to reverse the two branches should first ask which of the two results they would rather discover from a customer.

Proving Rules over Trust

Our encoded judgement creates a new obligation, because a bug in the rules would quietly corrupt every finding in the book. We cover all four branches with four synthetic cases, and each one starts from the same healthy baseline. The whole suite takes under a second and belongs in continuous integration alongside the validator from Chapter 3.

With that in place, here's the branch coverage test at **probes/test_verdict.py** and the run that follows:

```
"""Exercise every branch of the verdict rules."""
from pathlib import Path
from probes.envelope import load_envelopes
from probes.verdict import compare

env = load_envelopes(Path("signals/helpmate.yaml"))
base = {
    "ttft_p99_ms": 660.0, "tokens_per_second": 58.0, "recall_at_5":
0.80,
    "refusal_rate": 0.046, "override_rate": 0.050,
"escalation_rate": 0.018,
```

```
    "stream_completion_rate": 0.997, "tool_call_success": 0.972,
}

cases = {
    "absorbed": (dict(base, ttft_p99_ms=770.0), "accelerator"),
    "silent":   (dict(base, recall_at_5=0.63, override_rate=0.125),
"retrieval"),
    "degraded": (dict(base, tokens_per_second=43.6),
"accelerator"),
    "cascaded": (dict(base, tokens_per_second=43.6,
ttft_p99_ms=980.0,
                      stream_completion_rate=0.94,
override_rate=0.11), "accelerator"),
}

fails = 0
for expected, (inj, layer) in cases.items():
    got = compare(base, inj, env, layer)
    mark = "ok  " if got.verdict == expected else "FAIL"
    if got.verdict != expected:
        fails += 1
    print(f"{mark} expected={expected:<9} got={got.verdict:<9} "
          f"breached={got.breached}
layers={sorted(got.breached_layers)} reported={got.reported}")
raise SystemExit(fails)
```

All four branches resolve as designed, with the breached layers visible for inspection.

```
ok   expected=absorbed  got=absorbed  breached=[] layers=[]
reported=False
ok   expected=silent    got=silent    breached=['override_rate',
'recall_at_5'] layers=['boundary', 'retrieval'] reported=False
ok   expected=degraded  got=degraded
breached=['tokens_per_second'] layers=['accelerator'] reported=True
ok   expected=cascaded  got=cascaded  breached=['override_rate',
'stream_completion_rate', 'tokens_per_second', 'ttft_p99_ms']
layers=['accelerator', 'boundary', 'serving'] reported=True
```

Comparison Runner

A single command should now take us from two samples to a recorded result. Our runner accepts either capture paths or the word **`live`**, which lets the same tool serve offline analysis and cluster runs. Every field the findings table needs goes into a JSON record under **`results`**, so a table can be regenerated months later without anybody remembering what happened.

For now, we can write the runner at **probes/run_compare.py** like this:

```
"""Sample before and after, assign a verdict, and write one result
record."""
from __future__ import annotations

import argparse
import json
import time
from datetime import datetime, timezone
from pathlib import Path

from probes.envelope import load_envelopes
from probes.reduce import read_capture, reduce_signals
from probes.verdict import compare, deltas


def sample(source: str, endpoint: str) -> dict[str, float]:
    if source == "live":
        from probes.reduce_prom import
reduce_signals_from_prometheus

        return reduce_signals_from_prometheus(endpoint)
    return reduce_signals(read_capture(Path(source)))


def main() -> None:
    parser = argparse.ArgumentParser(description="Compare two
samples and record a verdict")
    parser.add_argument("--experiment", required=True)
    parser.add_argument("--layer", required=True)
    parser.add_argument("--baseline", required=True, help="capture
path or the word live")
    parser.add_argument("--injection", required=True, help="capture
path or the word live")
    parser.add_argument("--endpoint",
default="http://localhost:30090")
    parser.add_argument("--wait", type=int, default=0,
help="seconds between live samples")
    parser.add_argument("--signals",
default="signals/helpmate.yaml")
    args = parser.parse_args()

    envelopes = load_envelopes(Path(args.signals))
    before = sample(args.baseline, args.endpoint)
    if args.wait:
```

```
        time.sleep(args.wait)
    after = sample(args.injection, args.endpoint)

    outcome = compare(before, after, envelopes, args.layer)
    movement = deltas(before, after)

print(f"{'signal':<24}{'baseline':>11}{'injection':>11}{'delta':>10
}  status")
    print("-" * 68)
    for name in sorted(after):
        env = envelopes.get(name)
        mark = "-" if env is None else ("inside" if
env.holds(after[name]) else "BREACH")
        print(
            f"{name:<24}{before.get(name, float('nan')):>11}"
            f"{after[name]:>11}{movement.get(name, 0.0):>10}
{mark}"
        )
    print("-" * 68)
    print(f"injection layer : {args.layer}")
    print(f"breached layers : {sorted(outcome.breached_layers) or
'-'}")
    print(f"system reported : {outcome.reported}")
    print(f"VERDICT         : {outcome.verdict.upper()}")

    record = {
        "experiment_id": args.experiment,
        "ran_at":
datetime.now(timezone.utc).isoformat(timespec="seconds"),
        "injection_layer": args.layer,
        "observed_layers": sorted(outcome.breached_layers),
        "baseline": before,
        "injection": after,
        "deltas": movement,
        "breached": outcome.breached,
        "reported": outcome.reported,
        "verdict": outcome.verdict,
    }
    out = Path("results") / f"{args.experiment}.json"
    out.write_text(json.dumps(record, indent=2) + "\n",
encoding="utf-8")
    print(f"recorded        : {out}")
```

```
if __name__ == "__main__":
    main()
```

After this, every field the findings table needs now lands in one JSON record under **`results`**, which is what makes a table regenerable months later without anybody remembering the run. Our runner also refuses to guess: a missing signal raises rather than defaulting to zero, because a silently absent series was the exact trap that produced the fourth row of the Chapter 3 findings table. From here onward, every experiment in the book ends with this command rather than with a manual comparison.

Running Compute Experiments

Mild Throttle and First Signal Movement

Our first run cuts headroom to eighty seven percent, which corresponds roughly to a two hundred and sixty watt limit on a three hundred watt device. None of that reduction feels dramatic, and the result is more interesting because of it. We take a baseline from fifteen minutes of traffic before the cut, and the injection sample from fifteen minutes after it.

```
python3 -m probes.run_compare \
  --experiment exp-003a-throttle-mild --layer accelerator \
  --baseline results/healthy-capture.jsonl \
  --injection results/throttled-capture.jsonl
```

A single signal breaches, and the signal that did not breach carries the real finding.

```
signal                         baseline  injection     delta  status
--------------------------------------------------------------------
-
escalation_rate                  0.0175     0.0175       0.0  inside
override_rate                    0.0474     0.0474       0.0  inside
recall_at_5                      0.8035     0.8035       0.0  inside
refusal_rate                       0.05       0.05       0.0  inside
stream_completion_rate            0.995      0.995       0.0  inside
tokens_per_second                  57.9      50.38     -7.52  BREACH
tool_call_success                0.9711     0.9711       0.0  inside
ttft_p99_ms                       652.7      750.3      97.6  inside
--------------------------------------------------------------------
-
injection layer  : accelerator
breached layers  : ['accelerator']
system reported  : True
VERDICT          : DEGRADED
```

Consider what latency did during that run. The time to first token rose by ninety seven milliseconds and stayed comfortably inside its ceiling, while throughput fell straight through its floor. Any team monitoring latency alone would have seen a modest rise and concluded that the system was fine. Under compute starvation, throughput collapses before latency alerts fire, because a smaller batch still starts quickly and simply finishes slower. That single asymmetry justifies carrying **tokens_per_second** as a first class signal.

Hard Throttle and Cascade

A drop in headroom to fifty five percent changes the character of the failure entirely. Our second run holds everything else constant and only deepens the cut.

```
python3 -m probes.run_compare \
  --experiment exp-003b-throttle-hard --layer accelerator \
  --baseline results/healthy-capture.jsonl \
  --injection results/starved-capture.jsonl
```

```
stream_completion_rate         0.995     0.8525    -0.1425  BREACH
tokens_per_second               57.9      31.85     -26.05  BREACH
ttft_p99_ms                    652.7     1186.8      534.1  BREACH
----------------------------------------------------------------
-
injection layer : accelerator
breached layers : ['accelerator', 'serving']
system reported : True
VERDICT         : CASCADED
```

Here three signals breach across two layers, and streams begin timing out before completion. Our finding is that the accelerator layer has no gentle failure mode past roughly two thirds of nominal compute, since clients start abandoning responses rather than merely waiting longer. Our retrieval quality stayed untouched throughout both runs, which confirms that compute starvation is a throughput problem rather than a quality problem. In Chapter 5 we pick that thread up inside the serving layer, where the queue behaviour behind these numbers actually lives.

Draining Node under Load

Our third experiment leaves compute alone and removes a node instead. The Litmus library handles this one through the **node-drain** experiment, targeting the serving pool by label rather than by node name. The run has a prerequisite that catches people out, since the target node must be cordoned beforehand so that runner pods avoid landing on it. We attach two Prometheus probes to the engine, both reading their thresholds from the same envelopes the drift guard enforces.

So, the engine at **experiments/exp-004-node-drain.yaml** comes out like this:

```yaml
apiVersion: litmuschaos.io/v1alpha1
kind: ChaosEngine
metadata:
  name: exp-004-serving-node-drain
  namespace: helpmate-staging
spec:
  engineState: active
  annotationCheck: "false"
  chaosServiceAccount: litmus-admin
  jobCleanUpPolicy: retain
  appinfo:
    appns: helpmate-staging
    applabel: app=helpmate-inference
    appkind: deployment
  experiments:
    - name: node-drain
      spec:
        components:
          env:
            - name: NODE_LABEL
              value: "helpmate.io/pool=serving"
            - name: TOTAL_CHAOS_DURATION
              value: "180"
        probe:
          - name: recall-stays-above-floor
            type: promProbe
            mode: Continuous
            runProperties:
              probeTimeout: 5s
              interval: 15s
              retry: 2
            promProbe/inputs:
              endpoint: http://prometheus.observability.svc:9090
              query: avg(helpmate_recall_at_5)
              comparator:
                criteria: ">="
                value: "0.733"
          - name: ttft-stays-below-ceiling
            type: promProbe
            mode: Continuous
            runProperties:
              probeTimeout: 5s
              interval: 15s
              retry: 2
            promProbe/inputs:
```

```
            endpoint: http://prometheus.observability.svc:9090
            query: |
              histogram_quantile(0.99,
                sum by (le)
(rate(helpmate_ttft_seconds_bucket[2m]))) * 1000
            comparator:
              criteria: "<="
              value: "833.9"
```

The result surprised us, and the surprise is the most valuable thing in this chapter.

```
signal                         baseline  injection     delta  status
-------------------------------------------------------------------
-
escalation_rate                  0.0175      0.025    0.0075  inside
override_rate                    0.0474     0.0942    0.0468  BREACH
recall_at_5                      0.8035      0.695   -0.1085  BREACH
refusal_rate                       0.05      0.045    -0.005  inside
stream_completion_rate            0.995      0.995       0.0  inside
tokens_per_second                  57.9      57.93      0.03  inside
tool_call_success                0.9711     0.9714    0.0003  inside
ttft_p99_ms                       652.7      627.9     -24.8  inside
-------------------------------------------------------------------
-
injection layer  : accelerator
breached layers  : ['boundary', 'retrieval']
system reported  : False
VERDICT          : SILENT
```

Every infrastructure signal held, and two quality signals broke. The drain evicted a retriever replica, whose in memory rerank cache vanished along with it. The replacement came up healthy within twenty seconds and served worse results for several minutes while the cache refilled. Kubernetes reported a textbook success throughout, latency actually got slightly better under reduced load, and the support desk received measurably worse drafts. No standard reliability review would ever surface that outcome.

Stressing Pre-processing Path

Our fourth experiment applies CPU pressure to the retriever container using Chaos Mesh. Both tokenisation and embedding run on CPU, so the pre-processing path is where host contention actually bites. A ninety percent load across two workers for five minutes is aggressive without being absurd for a noisy neighbour scenario.

Next comes the stress definition, and here's what goes into **`experiments/exp-005-preprocess-stress.yaml`**:

```yaml
apiVersion: chaos-mesh.org/v1alpha1
kind: StressChaos
metadata:
  name: exp-005-preprocess-stress
  namespace: helpmate-staging
spec:
  mode: all
  duration: 300s
  selector:
    namespaces:
      - helpmate-staging
    labelSelectors:
      app: helpmate-retriever
  containerNames:
    - app
  stressors:
    cpu:
      workers: 2
      load: 90
```

The time to first token rose by thirty nine milliseconds and every envelope held, giving us an absorbed verdict. Our finding is that the CPU request and limit set in Chapter 3 leave adequate headroom for this workload. Such a result is worth recording precisely because it is dull, since an absorbed row tells a future engineer that this path was tested rather than overlooked.

Recording Findings

Findings Table

Our four experiments produced four different verdicts, which is unusual for a single chapter and useful for calibration.

Fault	Tool	Signal watched	Verdict	Finding
Power limit 300W to 260W, headroom 0.87	BYOC Job	tokens_per_second, ttft_p99_ms	Degraded	Throughput fell through its floor to 50.38 while latency rose only 97ms and stayed inside
Power limit 300W to 165W, headroom 0.55	BYOC Job	tokens_per_second, ttft_p99_ms, stream_completion_rate	Cascaded	Streams began timing out at 0.8525 completion; no gentle mode exists below two thirds nominal

Node drain, serving pool, under 8 req/s	Litmus	all eight signals	Silent	Evicted retriever lost its rerank cache; recall fell to 0.695 with every infrastructure signal healthy
CPU stress, 2 workers at 90 percent, retriever	Chaos Mesh	ttft_p99_ms, recall_at_5	Absorbed	Chapter 3 resource limits held; latency rose 39ms and nothing breached

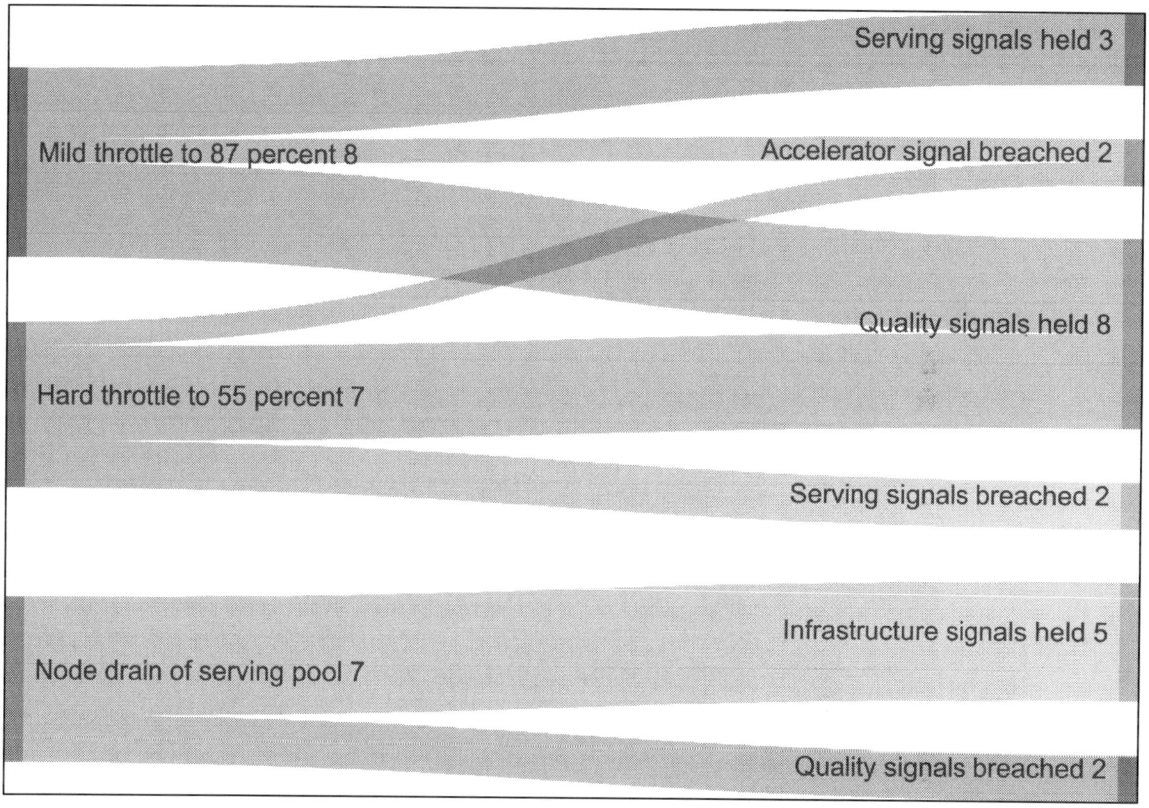

Our silent row is the one to carry forward. A node drain is among the most routine operations any platform team performs, scheduled during maintenance windows without a second thought. Nobody would classify it as a chaos experiment, and nobody would think to measure retrieval quality afterwards. In Chapter 5 we examine what happens inside the serving layer when the same kind of eviction lands on an inference replica holding a warm cache.

Summary

We moved below the layer where Kubernetes can rescue us. The starvation of compute offered no graceful path, so our injection script carried its own restore trap on three separate signals rather than trusting the platform to clean up. Our two throttle depths produced two different verdicts, and the milder one carried the sharper finding, since throughput fell through its floor while latency rose by less than a hundred milliseconds. A team alerting on latency alone would have missed the whole event.

Our comparison machinery arrived in this chapter and will carry the rest of the book. The four encoded rules now turn a before and after pair into one verdict without argument, and four synthetic cases prove every branch before we trust it on real runs. A routine node drain then produced our first genuine silent result, where an evicted retriever served degraded output for minutes while every infrastructure signal reported perfect health. In Chapter 5 we follow that eviction into the serving layer.

Chapter 5
Inference Serving Chaos

In Chapter 4 we ended with a node drain that evicted a retriever and produced our first genuine silent result. The starvation of compute turned out to be a throughput problem rather than a quality problem, and every experiment there pushed against hardware limits. We now move one layer up, into the serving engine itself, where the constraints are entirely software and the failure modes are considerably stranger.

Across this chapter, we will build a small continuous batching engine with a paged key value cache, then break it three separate ways. Our envelope file gains five new signals, because the original eight cannot see queue depth, cache pressure, or preemption at all. The three experiments that follow produce a degraded, a cascaded, and a silent verdict. Our closing sweep measures how admission queue depth trades visible rejections against invisible truncation, and the numbers are not what most teams expect.

What Constrains Inference Server?

Bottleneck Being Cache Over Queue

Most teams reason about an inference service the way they reason about a web service. In that picture requests arrive, a queue absorbs bursts, workers drain the queue, and capacity means workers. Such a model breaks immediately once generation enters the picture, because a request occupies memory for its entire lifetime rather than for one round trip. A conversation generating two hundred tokens holds its key value blocks across every one of those steps.

Our engine therefore has two independent limits, and only one of them behaves like a worker pool. The batch size caps how many streams the scheduler will run concurrently. The cache blocks cap how much total context those streams can hold between them. Whichever limit binds first determines the entire failure signature, and the cache almost always binds first with realistic prompt lengths. A four hundred token prompt at sixteen tokens per block consumes twenty seven blocks before generation even starts. Our preemption behaviour follows directly from that arithmetic. When a running request needs one more block and none remain, something has to yield, so the scheduler evicts a request and returns it to the queue. The recomputation then discards every token that request had already generated. That work performed and thrown away is the defining waste of an overloaded inference server, and no traditional queueing metric captures it. A dashboard showing healthy throughput can sit above a system recomputing the same responses four times each.

Mapping Model onto vLLM

A team running a real accelerator uses vLLM rather than our model, so the mapping between them matters. Exactly three quantities carry across directly. Our cache ratio corresponds to **`vllm:kv_cache_usage_perc`**, which reports the fraction of used blocks between zero and one. The queue depth corresponds to **`vllm:num_requests_waiting`**, and our preemption counter corresponds to **`vllm:num_preemptions_total`**. Every metric vLLM publishes carries the

vllm: prefix, with counters ending in **_total** as usual.

That substitution stays honest because we measure the same phenomena under different names. Our model reproduces admission, batching, block allocation, and recompute preemption, which is enough to generate every failure signature this chapter needs. The absolute numbers will differ on real hardware, and the shapes will not. A move to the accelerator path changes the queries in **reduce_prom.py** and leaves every envelope, probe, and verdict rule untouched.

Building Serving Model

Continuous Batching Engine

Our engine holds three collections, namely waiting, running, and done. Each tick admits whatever the cache can accommodate, generates tokens across the running set, then retires anything finished or expired. None of it is clever, and the lack of cleverness is deliberate, since a model we cannot reason about produces findings we cannot trust.

Our engine at **app/serving.py** takes the following shape:

```
"""A small continuous batching engine with a paged key value cache.

The CPU path runs this model. The accelerator path runs vLLM, which
exposes
the same quantities under the vllm: metric prefix.
"""
from __future__ import annotations

import math
import random
from dataclasses import dataclass, field


@dataclass
class Request:
    rid: int
    arrived: int
    prompt_tokens: int
    wanted_tokens: int
    generated: int = 0
    started: int | None = None
    finished: int | None = None
    preemptions: int = 0
    truncated: bool = False

    def blocks(self, block_tokens: int) -> int:
```

```
        return math.ceil((self.prompt_tokens + self.generated) /
block_tokens)


@dataclass
class EngineConfig:
    total_blocks: int = 1024
    block_tokens: int = 16
    max_batch: int = 24
    max_queue: int = 48
    token_budget: int = 64          # tokens the device can emit
per tick
    per_request_max: int = 1        # decode speed ceiling for one
stream
    timeout_ticks: int = 400


@dataclass
class Engine:
    cfg: EngineConfig = field(default_factory=EngineConfig)
    running: list[Request] = field(default_factory=list)
    waiting: list[Request] = field(default_factory=list)
    done: list[Request] = field(default_factory=list)
    rejected: int = 0
    accepted: int = 0
    preemptions: int = 0
    peak_block_use: int = 0

    def used_blocks(self) -> int:
        return sum(r.blocks(self.cfg.block_tokens) for r in
self.running)

    def cache_ratio(self) -> float:
        return round(self.used_blocks() / self.cfg.total_blocks, 4)

    def submit(self, req: Request) -> bool:
        if len(self.waiting) >= self.cfg.max_queue:
            self.rejected += 1
            return False
        self.waiting.append(req)
        self.accepted += 1
        return True

    def _free_blocks(self) -> int:
        return self.cfg.total_blocks - self.used_blocks()
```

```
    def _admit(self, tick: int) -> None:
        while self.waiting and len(self.running) <
self.cfg.max_batch:
            candidate = self.waiting[0]
            need = candidate.blocks(self.cfg.block_tokens)
            if need > self._free_blocks():
                break
            self.waiting.pop(0)
            candidate.started = tick
            self.running.append(candidate)

    def _preempt(self) -> None:
        # vLLM style recompute preemption: evict the newest request
entirely.
        victim = self.running.pop()
        victim.generated = 0
        victim.started = None
        victim.preemptions += 1
        self.preemptions += 1
        self.waiting.insert(0, victim)

    def restart(self) -> int:
        """What a rolling restart does to an engine mid flight,
cache included."""
        lost = len(self.running) + len(self.waiting)
        for req in self.running + self.waiting:
            req.truncated = True
            req.generated = 0
            req.finished = -1
            self.done.append(req)
        self.running.clear()
        self.waiting.clear()
        return lost

    def step(self, tick: int) -> None:
        self._admit(tick)
        if not self.running:
            return
        share = min(
            self.cfg.per_request_max,
            max(1, self.cfg.token_budget // max(len(self.running),
1)),
        )
        for req in list(self.running):
            for _ in range(share):
                if req.generated >= req.wanted_tokens:
```

```
                break
            before = req.blocks(self.cfg.block_tokens)
            req.generated += 1
            after = req.blocks(self.cfg.block_tokens)
            if after > before and self._free_blocks() < 0:
                req.generated -= 1
                self._preempt()
                break
        for req in list(self.running):
            expired = tick - req.arrived >= self.cfg.timeout_ticks
            if req.generated >= req.wanted_tokens or expired:
                req.truncated = req.generated < req.wanted_tokens
                req.finished = tick
                self.running.remove(req)
                self.done.append(req)
        self.peak_block_use = max(self.peak_block_use,
self.used_blocks())
```

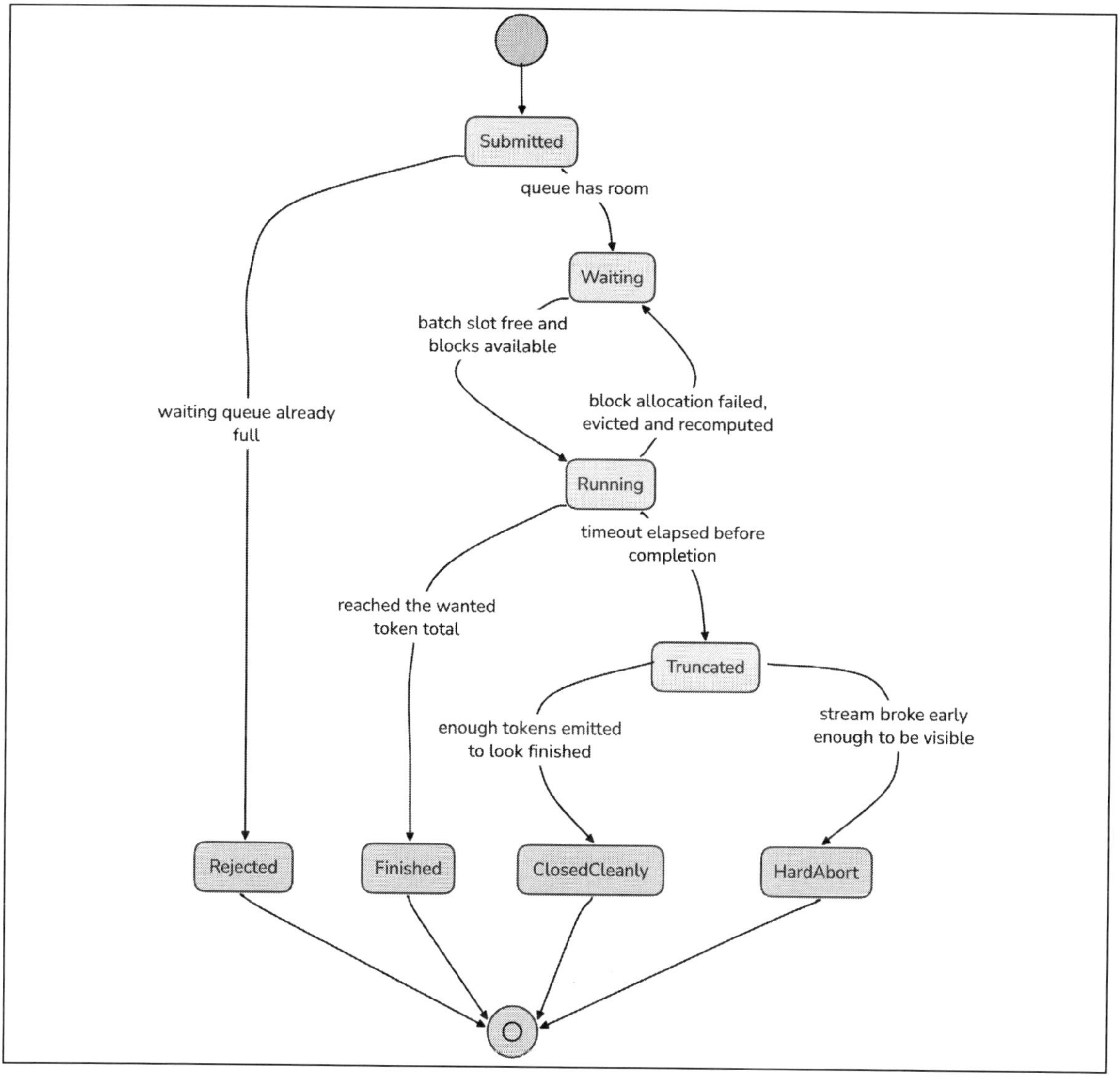

The careful study of the branch out of **`Truncated`** repays the effort, because that split produces the most dangerous result in this chapter. A stream cut short after eighty percent of its tokens closes cleanly at the transport layer, so the client receives a well formed response that simply stops mid thought. Only a stream broken early enough to look obviously wrong registers as a transport failure. Our **`stream_completion_rate`** signal watches transport, which means it cannot see the first case at all.

Capturing Runs Probes Can Read

Our harness converts an engine run into the same JSONL format our steady state work established, so every existing probe keeps working. We cover the scenarios we need with four profiles, differing only in arrival rate, queue depth, and whether a token cap applies. A single tick maps to 17.2 milliseconds, which puts single stream decode at roughly fifty eight tokens per second and keeps our numbers comparable with earlier chapters.

A rejected request gets a record too, marked with **admitted** set to false. That record matters more than it first appears, since admission rejections are invisible to any measurement taken inside the engine. A team reducing only served requests would report a healthy system while turning away a third of its traffic.

The capture harness at **probes/capture_serving.py** looks like this:

```
PROFILES = {
    "serving-nominal": {"rate": 0.10, "max_queue": 8, "max_batch":
24, "token_cap": 0},
    "serving-shed": {"rate": 0.20, "max_queue": 8, "max_batch": 24,
"token_cap": 0},
    "serving-unguarded": {"rate": 0.20, "max_queue": 400,
"max_batch": 64, "token_cap": 0},
    "serving-capped": {"rate": 0.10, "max_queue": 8, "max_batch":
24, "token_cap": 96},
}


def finished_record(req: Request, engine: Engine, rng:
random.Random) -> dict:
    wait_ticks = (req.started or req.arrived) - req.arrived
    service_ticks = max(1, (req.finished or 0) - (req.started or
0))
    intended = getattr(req, "intended_tokens", req.wanted_tokens)
    short = req.generated < intended
    # A stream that closes cleanly is complete at the transport
layer, even
    # when the content stopped early. Only a hard abort breaks the
transport.
    hard_abort = req.truncated and req.generated < 0.30 *
req.wanted_tokens
    looks_complete = short and not hard_abort
    return {
        "query_id": f"q{req.rid:05d}",
        "admitted": True,
        "queue_wait_ms": round(wait_ticks * TICK_MS, 1),
        "ttft_ms": round((wait_ticks + 1) * TICK_MS +
rng.uniform(40, 120), 1),
        "tokens_per_second": round(req.generated / (service_ticks *
TICK_MS / 1000.0), 2),
        "kv_cache_used_ratio": engine.cache_ratio(),
        "preempted": req.preemptions > 0,
```

```
        "truncated": short,
        "truncated_looks_complete": looks_complete,
        ...
    }
```

All four captures take a few seconds to generate.

```
for p in serving-nominal serving-shed serving-unguarded serving-capped; do
  python3 -m probes.capture_serving --profile "$p"
done
```

```
wrote results/serving-nominal-capture.jsonl with 406 records, 406 admitted
wrote results/serving-shed-capture.jsonl with 757 records, 519 admitted
wrote results/serving-unguarded-capture.jsonl with 709 records, 709 admitted
wrote results/serving-capped-capture.jsonl with 402 records, 402 admitted
```

Five New Signals for Serving Layer

What Missed by Existing Eight?

Our envelope file has served four chapters without modification, which is a reasonable run. Serving faults defeat it thoroughly. The cache pressure, queue depth, preemption, admission rejections, and quiet truncation all sit outside our original eight signals, and every one of them is a first class serving failure. New signals mid book are not a design flaw, since a measurement system that never grows is a measurement system nobody is using.

The first four belong to the serving layer, namely **`queue_wait_p99_ms`**, **`kv_cache_used_ratio`**, **`admission_reject_rate`**, and **`preemption_rate`**. Our fifth signal, **`truncated_valid_rate`**, belongs to the boundary layer instead, because it measures what the user received rather than what the engine did. The layer assignment is not cosmetic here, since the verdict rules from Chapter 4 treat serving breaches as reported and boundary breaches as potentially silent. That single placement decision determines whether a whole class of failure gets classified correctly. A truncation with a clean transport close produces no error anywhere in the infrastructure. Its detector placed in the serving layer would mark every such run as reported, and our silent category would quietly stop finding anything. A reader extending the signal file later should ask the same question first, namely whether a breach of the new signal would produce a visible symptom on its own.

Deriving and Committing New Envelopes

Our existing derivation script needs five new samplers and five new slack values. None of the method changes, since bootstrap bounds still supply precision and hand maintained slack still supplies tolerance. A single rule does change, and it deserves stating plainly. We derive only the new signals from this capture, leaving the original eight at their derived values, because a synthetic load harness is not a fair sample of production traffic.

That done, here's what gets appended to **probes/slack.yaml**:

```
admission_reject_rate: 0.03
kv_cache_used_ratio: 0.06
queue_wait_p99_ms: 250.0
preemption_rate: 0.02
truncated_valid_rate: 0.02
```

The derivation run against our nominal profile produces the proposed bounds.

```
python3 -m probes.derive --capture results/serving-nominal-
capture.jsonl
```

```
signal                          lo95       hi95     floor   ceiling
---------------------------------------------------------------------
admission_reject_rate            0.0        0.0         -      0.03
kv_cache_used_ratio           0.7388     0.7568         -    0.8168
queue_wait_p99_ms              430.0     807.54         -   1057.54
preemption_rate                  0.0        0.0         -      0.02
truncated_valid_rate             0.0        0.0         -      0.02
```

Exactly three of those bounds come out as pure slack, since a healthy engine never rejects, never preempts, and never truncates. Such envelopes look lazy and are exactly right, because the correct value for all three is zero and the slack only absorbs measurement noise. The cache utilisation behaves differently, sitting at roughly seventy five percent under nominal load with a ceiling at eighty two. A reader tempted to raise that ceiling should first observe what happens above it.

We then commit the five signals into **signals/helpmate.yaml**, bumping the schema to three.

```
serving:
  - signal: queue_wait_p99_ms
    floor: null
    ceiling: 1060.0
  - signal: kv_cache_used_ratio
    floor: null
    ceiling: 0.82
  - signal: admission_reject_rate
```

```
      floor: null
      ceiling: 0.03
    - signal: preemption_rate
      floor: null
      ceiling: 0.02
  boundary:
    - signal: truncated_valid_rate
      floor: null
      ceiling: 0.02
```

With this, the envelope file now carries thirteen signals across five layers at schema version three. Our drift guard covers the five additions automatically, since it compares the committed file against every probe threshold rather than against a list somebody maintains by hand. Anything that widens one of these ceilings after a noisy week will therefore fail continuous integration until the matching probe moves with it.

Three Experiments and Three Verdicts

Peak Load with Shedding Intact

Our first experiment doubles arrival rate against an engine whose admission queue holds eight requests. No other setting changes, and the shallow queue does precisely what a shallow queue is for.

```
python3 -m probes.run_compare \
  --experiment exp-006-peak-with-shedding --layer serving \
  --baseline results/serving-nominal-capture.jsonl \
  --injection results/serving-shed-capture.jsonl
```

```
signal                          baseline  injection     delta  status
---------------------------------------------------------------------
-
admission_reject_rate                0.0     0.3144    0.3144  BREACH
kv_cache_used_ratio                0.751     0.8018    0.0508  inside
preemption_rate                      0.0        0.0       0.0  inside
queue_wait_p99_ms                  599.4     1530.8     931.4  BREACH
stream_completion_rate               1.0        1.0       0.0  inside
truncated_valid_rate                 0.0     0.0019    0.0019  inside
ttft_p99_ms                        712.1     1631.6     919.5  BREACH
---------------------------------------------------------------------
-
injection layer : serving
breached layers : ['serving']
```

```
system reported : True
VERDICT         : DEGRADED
```

Nearly a third of arriving requests received a rejection, and every request the engine accepted got a complete response. The cache pressure barely moved, preemption never started, and truncation stayed at two tenths of one percent. Our system failed loudly and honestly under overload, which is the outcome a reliability review would call a success. All three breaches landed inside the serving layer, so the verdict resolves to degraded rather than cascaded.

Relaxing Admission Control

Our second experiment changes one setting. The queue depth rises from eight to four hundred, batch size rises alongside it, and the arrival rate stays exactly where the previous experiment left it. Many teams make this change deliberately, reasoning that rejecting customers is worse than making them wait.

```
python3 -m probes.run_compare \
  --experiment exp-007-admission-relaxed --layer serving \
  --baseline results/serving-nominal-capture.jsonl \
  --injection results/serving-unguarded-capture.jsonl
```

```
signal                        baseline  injection     delta  status
-------------------------------------------------------------------
-
admission_reject_rate              0.0        0.0       0.0  inside
kv_cache_used_ratio              0.751     0.9688    0.2178  BREACH
preemption_rate                    0.0     0.3427    0.3427  BREACH
queue_wait_p99_ms                599.4     4109.4    3510.0  BREACH
stream_completion_rate             1.0        1.0       0.0  inside
truncated_valid_rate               0.0     0.2299    0.2299  BREACH
ttft_p99_ms                      712.1     4187.2    3475.1  BREACH
-------------------------------------------------------------------
-
injection layer  : serving
breached layers  : ['boundary', 'serving']
system reported  : True
VERDICT          : CASCADED
```

The rejections fell to zero, which was the entire point of the change. Everything else fell apart. The cache utilisation climbed to ninety seven percent, more than a third of requests suffered at least one preemption, and time to first token rose past four seconds. Some twenty three percent of responses ended early while still closing cleanly, so nearly a quarter of users received a truncated draft that looked finished. The change did not remove the failure, and it converted a visible failure into an invisible one.

Token Cap Unreviewed

Our third experiment involves no load at all. Somebody sets a maximum generation length of ninety six tokens, perhaps to control spend, perhaps copied from a tutorial configuration. The arrival rate stays at nominal, the queue stays shallow, and the cluster has abundant capacity throughout.

```
python3 -m probes.run_compare \
  --experiment exp-008-token-cap --layer serving \
  --baseline results/serving-nominal-capture.jsonl \
  --injection results/serving-capped-capture.jsonl
```

```
signal                        baseline  injection     delta  status
-------------------------------------------------------------------
-
admission_reject_rate              0.0        0.0       0.0  inside
kv_cache_used_ratio              0.751     0.4277   -0.3233  inside
override_rate                   0.0718     0.0548    -0.017  inside
preemption_rate                    0.0        0.0       0.0  inside
queue_wait_p99_ms                599.4        0.0    -599.4  inside
recall_at_5                     0.8059     0.8092    0.0033  inside
refusal_rate                    0.0394     0.0473    0.0079  inside
stream_completion_rate             1.0        1.0       0.0  inside
tokens_per_second                58.53      58.77      0.24  inside
tool_call_success               0.9802     0.9881    0.0079  inside
truncated_valid_rate               0.0     0.9428    0.9428  BREACH
ttft_p99_ms                      712.1      136.3    -575.8  inside
-------------------------------------------------------------------
-
injection layer : serving
breached layers : ['boundary']
system reported : False
VERDICT         : SILENT
```

That column of deltas deserves a slow read. The time to first token fell by 576 milliseconds. The queue wait dropped to zero, cache pressure halved, and throughput ticked upward. Every operational dashboard in the building turned a healthier shade of green. Meanwhile ninety four percent of responses stopped mid sentence and closed the stream cleanly, so the support desk received truncated drafts all day with no signal anywhere that anything had changed.

Such a fault would survive indefinitely in most organisations. Nobody investigates a service whose latency dropped, and the override rate rise takes weeks to become statistically obvious against normal variation. Our single boundary layer signal caught it in a fifteen minute window, which is the entire return on our steady state work. In Chapter 6 we find a closely related failure one layer down, where a model version changes without anybody publishing a release.

Insights by Queue Depth Sweep

Goodput Moves and Honesty Collapses

Our two experiments suggested a trade off between rejections and truncation, and a sweep settles the question properly. Our script holds arrival rate at 0.20 and varies queue depth across two orders of magnitude, reporting delivered responses as a fraction of everything submitted.

```
python3 -m probes.queue_sweep --rate 0.20
```

max_queue	reject	truncated	preempt	waitP99	delivered	goodput
4	31.9%	0.0%	0	1032ms	505	64.5%
8	30.5%	0.0%	0	1531ms	514	65.6%
12	30.8%	0.6%	0	2116ms	504	64.4%
16	30.8%	1.8%	0	2528ms	495	63.2%
24	27.7%	13.7%	0	3509ms	448	57.2%
48	2.3%	27.2%	442	4334ms	513	65.5%
120	0.0%	31.6%	448	4489ms	491	62.7%
400	0.0%	31.6%	448	4489ms	491	62.7%

The last column deserves attention first, because it demolishes the usual argument. The goodput sits between 57 and 66 percent across every queue depth, with no meaningful trend. A hundredfold deeper queue delivered no additional successful responses whatsoever. Every request the deep queue accepted instead of rejecting came back as a truncated response, a preemption, or a four second wait.

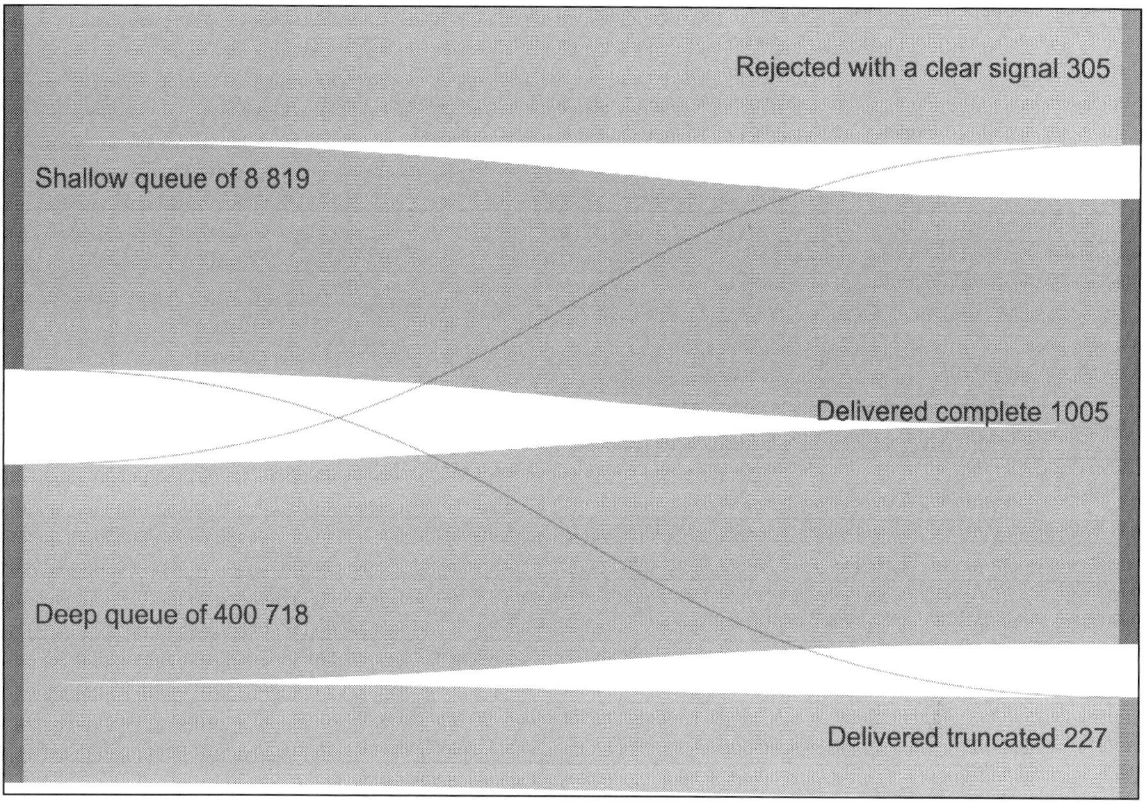

The admission control does not buy throughput. What it buys is honesty about failure, and that is a far more valuable thing to purchase. A rejection arrives as a status code the caller can retry, log, and alert on. A truncation arrives as a two hundred response containing a plausible draft that stops early. Both represent the same underlying shortage of capacity, and only one of them will ever appear in an incident review.

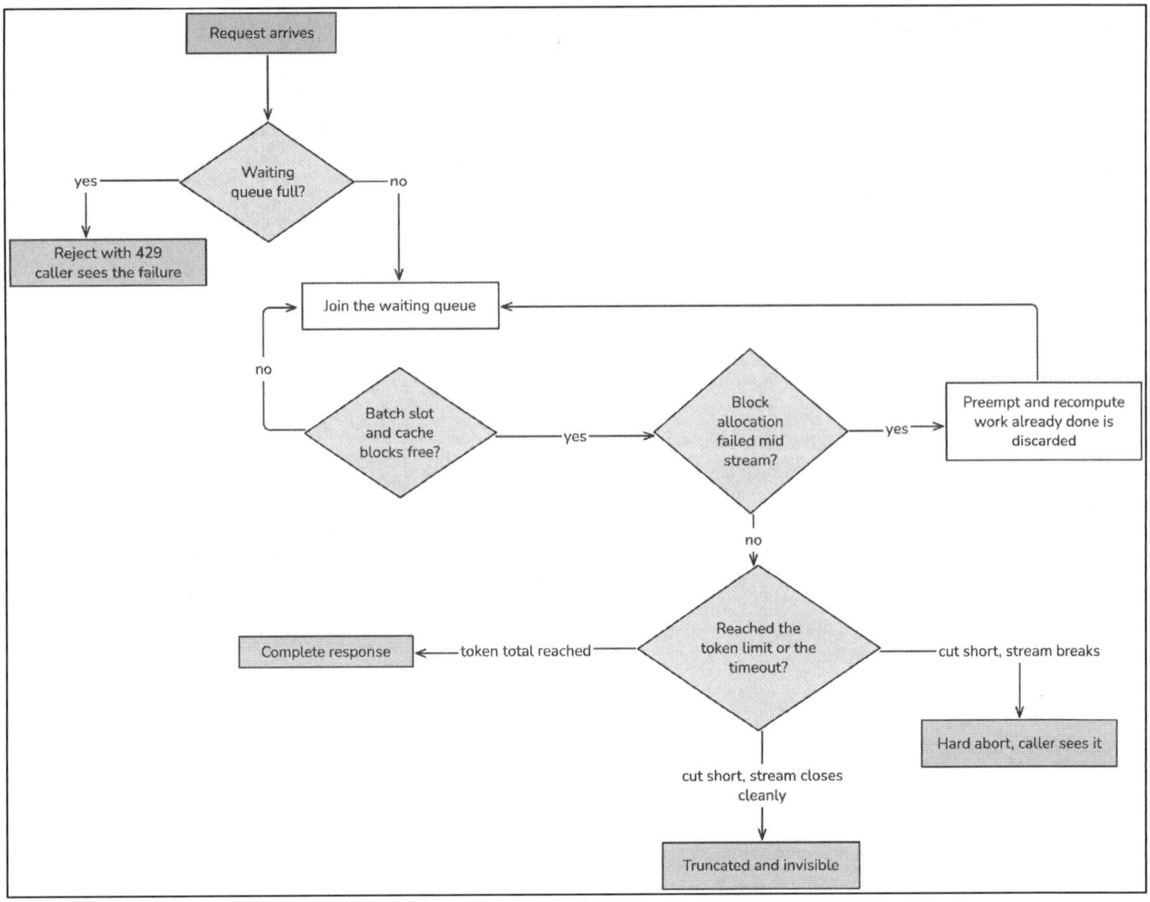

Recording Findings

Fault	Tool	Signal watched	Verdict	Finding
Arrival rate doubled, queue depth 8	Load harness	admission_reject_rate, queue_wait_p99_ms, ttft_p99_ms	Degraded	31.4 percent rejected, zero truncation, every accepted request completed
Queue depth raised from 8 to 400	Config change	kv_cache_used_ratio, preemption_rate, truncated_valid_rate	Cascaded	Rejections reached zero while 34 percent of requests suffered preemption and 23 percent truncated
Generation capped at 96 tokens	Config change	truncated_valid_rate	Silent	94.3 percent truncated cleanly while latency fell 576ms and every other signal held
Queue depth	Load	delivered fraction	Absorbed	Goodput held between

swept from 4 to 400	harness			57 and 66 percent regardless of depth, so depth changes the failure mode rather than the capacity

Our silent row is the one to carry into a design review. Every organisation running an inference service has a maximum token setting somewhere, usually inherited from a default nobody chose deliberately. No standard deployment pipeline would flag that value as a reliability control, and no standard monitoring stack would notice when it starts biting.

Summary

We built a continuous batching engine small enough to reason about and faithful enough to break in realistic ways. The binding constraint turned out to be cache blocks rather than batch slots, and preemption turned out to be the waste nobody measures. Our envelope file gained five new signals, four in the serving layer and one deliberately placed in the boundary layer, because that placement determines whether quiet truncation ever gets classified as silent.

Our three experiments produced three different verdicts from the same engine. The peak load with a shallow queue failed loudly and delivered complete responses to everyone it accepted. A relaxed admission control removed every rejection and converted them into preemptions, four second waits, and truncated drafts. A token cap nobody reviewed then produced our cleanest silent result yet, where latency fell by more than half a second while ninety four percent of responses stopped mid sentence. In Chapter 6 we move to the artifact layer, where a model version can change without any release taking place.

CHAPTER 6

MODEL ARTIFACTS, REGISTRIES, AND VERSION SKEW

In Chapter 5 we closed with a token cap that nobody reviewed, where ninety four percent of responses stopped mid sentence while every operational dashboard turned a healthier shade of green. Such a fault lived entirely in configuration. We now move one layer down, to the artifacts that configuration points at, where the equivalent failures are harder to see and considerably harder to reverse.

Across this chapter, we will read a safetensors file without loading it, discover a corruption class our structural checks cannot detect, and close that hole with a manifest. Our golden set then gets scored against two model versions, producing a release that passes its own gate while collapsing on the highest risk category. A pair of Chaos Mesh definitions follow, one corrupting weights on read and one throttling the object store. The four experiments produce four verdicts, and one earlier layer assignment gets corrected along the way.

Why Artifact Layer Fails?

Artifact Are Not Container Image

Our industry learned a set of habits from container images that transfer badly to model weights. An image carries a content addressed digest, so pulling the wrong one is arithmetically impossible. A registry verifies that digest on every pull, and orchestrators refuse to start a container whose layers fail verification. None of that machinery extends to the multi gigabyte tensor file the container downloads after it starts. Our weights arrive through a separate path with separate assumptions. An object store hands over bytes, a loader parses them, and a serving engine begins answering requests. Between those three steps sit several failure modes that produce no error at all. A partial read yields a shorter file, a corrupted region yields plausible garbage, and a version pointer edited in a configuration map yields entirely different behaviour. Every one of them ends with a healthy pod serving traffic.

The reversibility differs as well, which changes how we design experiments here. A rollback of a bad image restores exactly the previous bytes. A rollback of a bad model restores the previous weights and leaves behind every response the new version already produced, along with whatever downstream systems did with them. We therefore treat detection speed as the primary property at this layer, since the damage accumulates from the moment the artifact starts serving.

Correcting Layer Assignment

A correction belongs at the front of this chapter rather than buried in it. We originally placed **`model_version_drift`** in the artifact layer, alongside registry availability and cold start duration. That placement looked natural, since a version change is obviously an artifact event. Our verdict rules show why it was wrong. Our reporting layers determine whether a breach counts as visible. The artifact breaches sit in that set because a registry timeout or a failed weight load produces an error somebody can see. A version drift produces nothing of the sort, because the new artifact loads perfectly and serves confidently. The signal left in the artifact layer would mark every version regression as reported, and our silent category would stop catching the exact failure it exists for.

In Chapter 5 we made the same judgement correctly for **truncated_valid_rate**, which measures what the user received rather than what the engine did. That rule applied consistently moves **model_version_drift** into the boundary layer and adds **golden_set_score** beside it. The two remaining artifact signals stay where they belong, namely **cold_start_seconds** and a new **artifact_integrity_failures**. Our schema version rises to four, and the reasoning gets written into the commit message rather than into somebody's memory.

Verifying Loader

Reading 'safetensors'

Our verification should happen before a loader touches the file, since a loader with sixteen gigabytes of weights already in memory has passed the point of cheap failure. Fortunately the safetensors format makes early verification easy. The first eight bytes hold a little endian unsigned integer giving the header length. That many bytes of JSON follow, mapping each tensor name to a dtype, a shape, and a pair of byte offsets into the data buffer that comes afterwards.

The layout yields three checks immediately. Our declared header length must be plausible and must fit inside the file. Our header must parse as JSON. Finally, the file size must equal eight plus the header length plus the largest end offset any tensor declares. A fourth check scans the payload for improbably long runs of zero bytes, which is what a partial write or a zero filling corruption leaves behind.

Here's what the verifier at **probes/artifact_check.py** needs to hold:

```
"""Verify a safetensors artifact is whole before anything tries to
load it."""
from __future__ import annotations

import argparse
import hashlib
import json
import struct
from dataclasses import dataclass
from pathlib import Path

HEADER_PREFIX = 8       # bytes holding the little endian header
length
MAX_HEADER = 100_000_000


@dataclass
```

```
class Finding:
    check: str
    ok: bool
    detail: str


def inspect(path: Path, zero_run_limit: int = 4096, manifest: dict
| None = None) -> list[Finding]:
    findings: list[Finding] = []
    size = path.stat().st_size
    if size < HEADER_PREFIX:
        return [Finding("prefix", False, f"file is {size} bytes,
shorter than the header prefix")]

    with path.open("rb") as handle:
        header_len = struct.unpack("<Q",
handle.read(HEADER_PREFIX))[0]
        if header_len == 0 or header_len > MAX_HEADER or header_len
+ HEADER_PREFIX > size:
            return [Finding("header-length", False, f"declared
header of {header_len} bytes is impossible")]
        findings.append(Finding("header-length", True,
f"{header_len} bytes"))

        raw = handle.read(header_len)
        try:
            header = json.loads(raw)
        except json.JSONDecodeError as exc:
            return findings + [Finding("header-json", False,
f"header did not parse, {exc}")]
        findings.append(Finding("header-json", True,
f"{len(header)} entries"))

        tensors = {k: v for k, v in header.items() if k !=
"__metadata__"}
        end = max((v["data_offsets"][1] for v in tensors.values()),
default=0)
        expected = HEADER_PREFIX + header_len + end
        whole = expected == size
        findings.append(
            Finding("file-size", whole, f"expected {expected}
bytes, found {size}")
        )
        if not whole:
            return findings
```

```
        handle.seek(HEADER_PREFIX + header_len)
        digest = hashlib.sha256()
        longest_zero_run = run = 0
        while chunk := handle.read(1 << 20):
            digest.update(chunk)
            for byte in chunk:
                run = run + 1 if byte == 0 else 0
                longest_zero_run = max(longest_zero_run, run)
        findings.append(Finding("payload-sha256", True,
digest.hexdigest()[:16]))
        findings.append(
            Finding(
                "zero-run",
                longest_zero_run < zero_run_limit,
                f"longest run of zero bytes is {longest_zero_run}",
            )
        )
    return findings
```

A verifier tested against healthy input proves very little, so we damage three copies of a known good file. The first copy gets truncated to seventy two percent of its length, imitating an interrupted transfer. Another has twenty thousand bytes in the middle replaced with zeros, imitating the corruption Chaos Mesh produces later in this chapter. A third has a single byte altered inside the JSON header.

```
python3 -m probes.artifact_check artifacts/model-
truncated.safetensors
```

```
pass   header-length   228 bytes
pass   header-json     3 entries
FAIL   file-size       expected 524524 bytes, found 377657
3 check(s), 1 failure(s)
```

Case Structural Checks Missed

The first two damaged copies fail immediately, and the third passes every check.

```
python3 -m probes.artifact_check artifacts/model-
badheader.safetensors
```

```
pass   header-length   228 bytes
pass   header-json     3 entries
pass   file-size       expected 524524 bytes, found 524524
pass   payload-sha256  4aa7383170dce2a1
```

```
pass  zero-run        longest run of zero bytes is 0
5 check(s), 0 failure(s)
```

Our altered byte landed inside a tensor name and happened to leave the JSON valid. Every offset stayed correct, the file size stayed correct, and the payload stayed byte identical. A loader reading this file finds a tensor called something slightly wrong, which either raises a missing key error somewhere deep in model construction or, in a loader tolerant of extra keys, silently leaves one tensor uninitialised. No structural verification can catch that class, because nothing about the structure is broken.

The hole needs external truth rather than better parsing. Our fix records a manifest at build time, pinning the whole file digest alongside the sorted set of tensor names. Any later verification compares against that record instead of relying on internal consistency alone. Such a manifest costs one command to produce and belongs in the same artifact repository as the weights.

Having settled that, we generate the manifest and re-run the failing case:

```
python3 -m probes.artifact_check artifacts/model-v1.safetensors \
  --write-manifest artifacts/model-v1.manifest.json
python3 -m probes.artifact_check artifacts/model-
badheader.safetensors \
  --manifest artifacts/model-v1.manifest.json
```

The two additional checks now run, and both of them fire.

```
pass  file-size       expected 524524 bytes, found 524524
pass  payload-sha256  4aa7383170dce2a1
pass  zero-run        longest run of zero bytes is 0
FAIL  tensor-names    3 names, expected 3
FAIL  manifest-sha256 a68ae74fa4b9f3f6 against f6111147778212ec
7 check(s), 2 failure(s)
```

Measuring Behavioural Delta between Versions

Scoring Golden Set by Category

Our golden set has existed since we first defined steady state, as four hundred questions with confirmed responses. An aggregate score served us adequately while we were breaking infrastructure. A version comparison needs more resolution than an aggregate can provide, because a model release rarely gets uniformly worse. A release trades capability, so one category improves while another quietly falls apart.

We therefore group the set into five categories carrying different business risk. The settlement and refund questions sit at high risk, since a wrong response there costs money directly. The webhook and API error questions sit at medium risk. Billing questions sit at low risk, because the support desk catches those errors trivially. Our composition follows traffic volume, which is how most teams build a set, and Chapter 6 exists partly to show what that choice costs.

With that in place, the golden set builder at **`probes/golden_set.py`** looks like this:

```
"""Build and load the HelpMate golden set, grouped by business risk
category."""
from __future__ import annotations

import json
import random
from pathlib import Path

# Sampled by traffic volume, which is how most teams build a golden
set.
# Chapter 6 shows why weighting by business risk instead would be
wiser.
CATEGORIES = {
    "settlements": 40,
    "refunds": 60,
    "webhooks": 90,
    "api_errors": 100,
    "billing": 110,
}
RISK = {"settlements": "high", "refunds": "high", "webhooks":
"medium",
        "api_errors": "medium", "billing": "low"}
DEFAULT_PATH = Path("probes/golden-set.jsonl")


def build(path: Path = DEFAULT_PATH, seed: int = 3) -> int:
    rng = random.Random(seed)
    written = 0
    path.parent.mkdir(parents=True, exist_ok=True)
    with path.open("w", encoding="utf-8") as handle:
        for category, total in CATEGORIES.items():
            for index in range(total):
                written += 1
                handle.write(
                    json.dumps(
                        {
                            "qid": f"{category[:3]}-{index:03d}",
                            "category": category,
                            "risk": RISK[category],
                            "unanswerable": rng.random() < 0.10,
```

```
                                "confirmed_on": "2026-07-01",
                            }
                        )
                        + "\n"
                    )
    return written
```

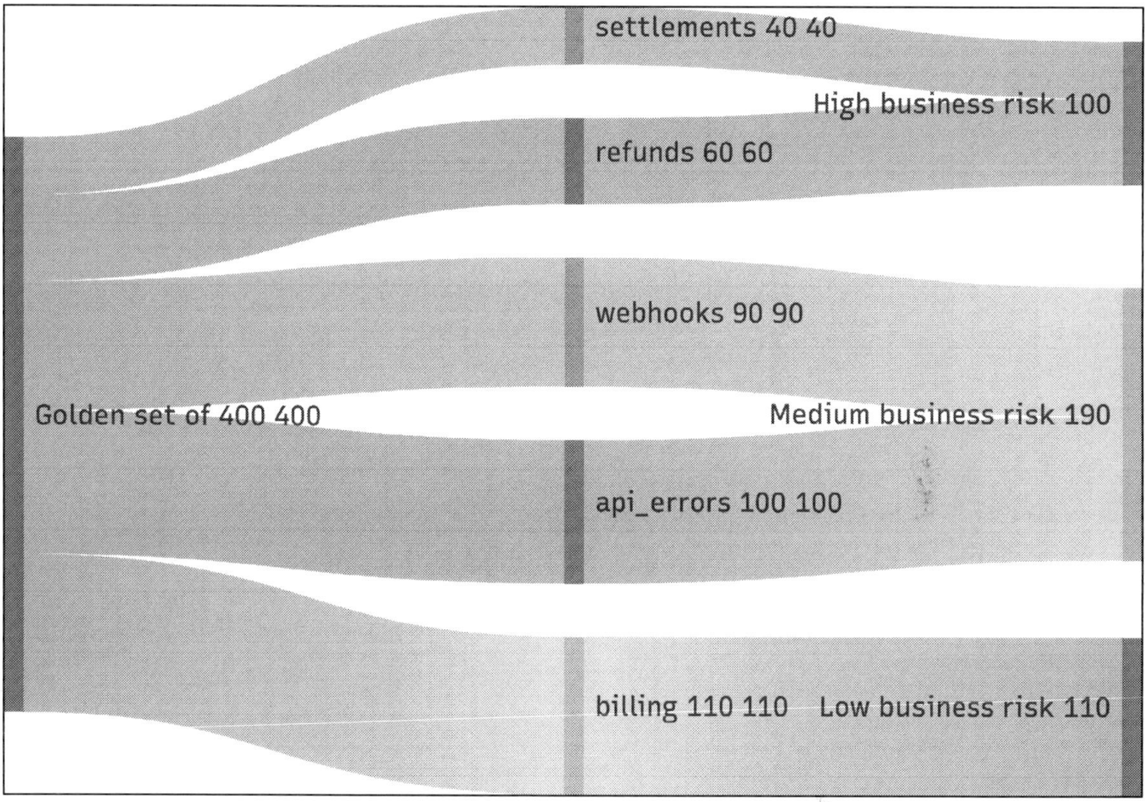

The mismatch in that view is obvious. A hundred of our four hundred questions cover high risk behaviour, while one hundred and ten cover the category whose errors matter least. The weighting by volume produced that shape honestly, since billing questions genuinely arrive most often. Any aggregate computed across the whole set therefore gives our lowest stakes category more influence than our highest stakes one.

Release That Passed Its Own Gate

Our comparison harness scores the set against two versions and reports per category. The 1.4.0 release represents what production serves today, and 1.5.0 represents the candidate. No part of the harness knows which release anybody prefers.

We follow that by running the following comparison:

```
python3 -m probes.version_delta --from-version 1.4.0 --to-version
1.5.0
```

The per category breakdown tells a very different story from the overall figure.

```
category        risk          1.4.0     1.5.0     delta   status
------------------------------------------------------------------
api_errors      medium         0.92      0.96      0.04   held
billing         low          0.9273    0.9909    0.0636   held
refunds         high         0.9167      0.95    0.0333   held
settlements     high          0.925       0.6    -0.325   REGRESSED
webhooks        medium       0.8889    0.9556    0.0667   held
------------------------------------------------------------------
overall                       0.915      0.93     0.015

golden_set_score     : 0.93
model_version_drift : 1
regressed categories: settlements
```

The overall row comes first, because that is the number a release gate would check. The aggregate accuracy rose by one and a half points, so any threshold gate comparing overall scores approves this release without hesitation. A full four categories genuinely got better, and the release notes would be entirely accurate in saying so. The settlement questions meanwhile fell from 0.925 to 0.600, which means two responses in five about failed settlements are now wrong.

The same comparison restricted to the high risk subset makes the damage visible in one number.

```
high risk subset, 100 questions
  1.4.0 0.92    1.5.0 0.81    delta -0.11
```

A pair of conclusions follow, and both are actionable. Our release gate must compare per category rather than in aggregate, since an aggregate can only ever hide a trade. Our golden set composition should also be reweighted toward business risk instead of traffic volume, because forty questions cannot detect a subtle regression reliably. Both changes cost an afternoon and would have caught this release before it shipped.

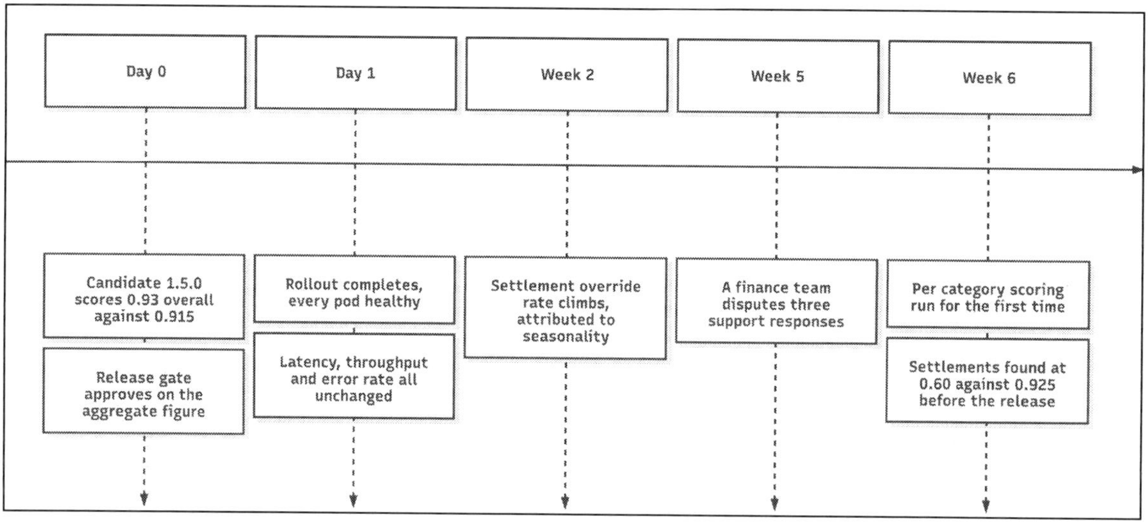

Starving Artifact Path

Corrupting Weights with IOChaos

In Chapter 5 we used Chaos Mesh for network faults, and the artifact layer needs its filesystem faults instead. The tool offers four actions, namely **`latency`**, **`fault`**, **`attrOverride`**, and **`mistake`**. Our interest lies in the last of those, since **`mistake`** replaces bytes during read or write operations rather than failing the call outright. A fill of zeros over a bounded length reproduces exactly the corruption class our verifier now catches.

A warning from the upstream documentation deserves repeating, because it applies with unusual force here. The IOChaos resource can damage data, and pointing it at a volume holding anything you cannot recreate is a poor idea. Our weights volume is a cache populated from the object store, so corrupting it costs a re-download and nothing more. A reader tempted to aim this at a persistent volume should reconsider first.

For now, we can write the corruption definition at **`experiments/exp-010-weights-corruption.yaml`** like this:

```
apiVersion: chaos-mesh.org/v1alpha1
kind: IOChaos
metadata:
  name: exp-010-weights-corruption
  namespace: helpmate-staging
spec:
  action: mistake
  mode: one
  duration: 120s
```

```
selector:
  namespaces:
    - helpmate-staging
  labelSelectors:
    app: helpmate-inference
volumePath: /var/lib/helpmate/weights
path: /var/lib/helpmate/weights/**/*.safetensors
mistake:
  filling: zero
  maxOccurrences: 2
  maxLength: 20000
methods:
  - READ
```

That definition applied while a replica restarts produces a read the verifier rejects. Our pod then refuses to become ready, an alert fires, and **artifact_integrity_failures** rises above its ceiling of zero. Such an outcome is the good case, since the corruption never reached a served response.

Pull Storms and Cold Start Amplification

The cold start behaviour changes character entirely once several replicas restart together. A single replica pulling sixteen gigabytes from a store serving nine hundred mebibytes per second finishes in well under a minute. All eight replicas pulling simultaneously share that same bandwidth, so each one takes eight times as long. No part of the store failed, and every replica waits.

From here we model the amplification at **probes/coldstart.py**, and here's the file with the run that follows:

```
python3 -m probes.coldstart --weights-gib 16 --store-mib-s 900 --
throttled-mib-s 180
```

The table shows how quickly the ceiling of one hundred and twenty seconds falls away.

```
artifact 16.0 GiB, ceiling 120.0s
 pullers   warm cache   cold, full   cold, throttled
----------------------------------------------------
       1       18.0s        36.2s           109.0s
       2       18.0s        54.4s           200.0s*
       4       18.0s        90.8s           382.1s*
       8       18.0s       163.6s*          746.2s*
      12       18.0s       236.5s*         1110.3s*
      16       18.0s       309.3s*         1474.4s*
----------------------------------------------------
* exceeds the cold_start_seconds ceiling of 120.0s
```

The two columns matter more than the numbers inside them. A warm cache restart completes in eighteen seconds regardless of how many replicas restart, since nothing crosses the network at all. A cold restart scales linearly with the number of simultaneous pullers, so the difference between a rolling restart and a simultaneous one is the difference between eighteen seconds and five minutes. Any engineer who has drained a node pool during an incident has met this behaviour without recognising it.

A throttle on the store makes the point sharper still. Our third column applies a bandwidth limit of one hundred and eighty mebibytes per second, which Chaos Mesh produces with the **bandwidth** action. Even a single replica then takes one hundred and nine seconds, sitting inside the ceiling by eleven seconds. A second replica breaches it. Such a narrow margin under a single fault is the definition of a system with no headroom.

Four Experiments, Four Verdicts

Running Comparison

Our comparison runner needs one addition for this chapter. A pair of signals now gets measured outside the request capture, since a golden set score and an integrity check result do not appear in per request telemetry. A merge option keeps one code path rather than forking the tool.

We continue by running all four artifact experiments as below:

```
python3 -m probes.run_compare --experiment exp-012-version-skew --
layer artifact \
  --baseline results/serving-nominal-capture.jsonl \
  --injection results/serving-nominal-capture.jsonl \
  --add-baseline golden_set_score=0.915 --add-baseline
model_version_drift=0 \
  --add-injection golden_set_score=0.930 --add-injection
model_version_drift=1
```

Our version skew run produces the result this chapter was written for.

```
signal                          baseline  injection     delta  status
----------------------------------------------------------------------
-
golden_set_score                   0.915       0.93     0.015  inside
model_version_drift                  0.0        1.0       1.0  BREACH
refusal_rate                      0.0394     0.0394       0.0  inside
stream_completion_rate               1.0        1.0       0.0  inside
tokens_per_second                  58.53      58.53       0.0  inside
truncated_valid_rate                 0.0        0.0       0.0  inside
ttft_p99_ms                        712.1      712.1       0.0  inside
```

```
--------------------------------------------------------------------
-
injection layer : artifact
breached layers : ['boundary']
system reported : False
VERDICT         : SILENT
```

The **`golden_set_score`** entry in that output deserves attention. Our aggregate quality signal sits comfortably inside its floor, having risen rather than fallen. Only the per category drift detector breaches, and it breaches in the boundary layer where nothing reports it. Had we left that signal in the artifact layer where it was originally placed, this run would have been classified as degraded and the whole point would have been lost.

Recording Findings

Fault	Tool	Signal watched	Verdict	Finding
Rolling restart, warm node cache	kubectl	cold_start_seconds, ttft_p99_ms	Absorbed	Eighteen second starts regardless of replica number, no network transfer involved
Weights zero filled on read, 20KB	Chaos Mesh IOChaos	artifact_integrity_failures	Degraded	Verifier rejected the artifact, pod refused readiness, corruption never reached a response
Eight replicas pulling 16 GiB together	Chaos Mesh NetworkChaos	cold_start_seconds, admission_reject_rate	Cascaded	Cold start reached 163.6s against a 120s ceiling, surviving replicas then shed 31 percent of traffic
Model version 1.4.0 replaced by 1.5.0	Config change	model_version_drift, golden_set_score	Silent	Aggregate score rose 1.5 points while settlements fell from 0.925 to 0.600
Single byte altered inside the JSON header	Manual	artifact_integrity_failures	Silent	Every structural check passed; only the recorded manifest caught it

The two silent rows in that table are unusual and instructive. Both share a shape, since both involve an artifact that is internally consistent and externally wrong. No part of the file, the pod, or the cluster can detect either one, because detection requires comparison against something recorded earlier. In Chapter 7 we find the same shape again in the retrieval layer, where an index can be perfectly healthy and thoroughly out of date.

Summary

We built a verifier that reads a safetensors header without loading a single tensor, then proved it against three deliberately damaged files. The first two failed immediately, and the third exposed a class of corruption no structural check can reach, since a renamed tensor leaves the file perfectly self consistent. A manifest recorded at build time closed that hole, which is a reminder that internal consistency and correctness are different properties.

Our golden set then gained categories and business risk labels, and scoring two model versions against it produced the sharpest finding so far. The aggregate accuracy rose by one and a half points while settlement responses collapsed from 0.925 to 0.600, so a release gate checking the aggregate would approve the regression without hesitation. Our four experiments produced four verdicts, two of them silent, and one earlier layer assignment got corrected to make that classification possible. In Chapter 7 we move into retrieval.

Chapter 7

Retrieval and Context Chaos

In Chapter 6 we ended with two silent rows in the same table, both sharing a shape. An artifact that is internally consistent and externally wrong cannot be detected from the inside, because detection requires comparison against something recorded earlier. The retrieval layer produces the same shape at greater scale and with greater frequency, since an index goes out of date every single day whether anybody touches it or not.

Across this chapter, we will build a vector index small enough to reason about and degrade it three separate ways. Our central question is whether retrieval is helping at all, which we settle by scoring every scenario against a no retrieval baseline. We then test similarity based abstention properly, and find it protects against two failure modes while remaining structurally blind to the third. The five experiments that follow add two new signals to the envelope file, and one property of our verdict rules turns out to be a genuine finding rather than a limitation.

Retrieval Not Reporting Its Failure

Three Ways Retrieval Goes Wrong

Our retrieval layer fails in three distinct ways, and conflating them produces confused experiments. An availability failure removes documents from the index, whether through a killed replica, a lost shard, or an incomplete restore. A compatibility failure leaves every document present while making the query unable to find them, which happens whenever the embedding model at query time no longer matches the one used at ingest. A freshness failure leaves everything present and findable while the content itself has moved on. Only the first of those three resembles a conventional outage. A missing shard produces fewer results, lower similarity scores, and eventually visible errors, so ordinary operational instinct applies. The compatibility case behaves similarly from a signal perspective, since a query embedded in the wrong space matches nothing well. Both produce a system that visibly cannot find things.

The freshness case behaves in the opposite direction entirely. Our index still holds a document that matches the query beautifully, scores highly, and reaches the prompt with full confidence. No part of the retrieval operation went wrong, because the operation retrieved exactly what it was asked for. Only the content is out of date, and content currency is not a property any vector store measures. Such a failure produces better looking telemetry than a healthy system under load.

Layer with No Voice

A property of our verdict rules deserves stating before we run anything, because it emerged from this chapter rather than being designed into it. We established earlier that a verdict of degraded requires two conditions, namely that the system reported the breach and that breaches stayed inside the injection layer. The reporting layers are accelerator, serving, and artifact, since each surfaces failure through ordinary errors. Our retrieval layer sits outside that set deliberately. A vector store returning poor results returns them successfully, with a two hundred status and a well formed payload. Both conditions applied to a retrieval injection therefore produce an impossible combination, since retrieval cannot report its own failure and any symptom that does surface has already reached the boundary layer. Our rules make degraded unreachable for this layer.

That discovery felt at first like a modelling error and turned out to be the most useful thing the rules have told us. Every retrieval fault is either absorbed entirely, silent, or has already reached the user by the time anything complains. No middle ground exists where the system notices its own retrieval problem and contains it. A team designing retrieval observability should treat that absence as the requirement, rather than assuming a monitoring gap they can close with another dashboard.

Building Breakable Index

Corpus, Index, and Ground Truth

Our model needs three separable pieces, and keeping them separate is what makes freshness failures expressible at all. A corpus holds documents, each carrying a topic, a vector, and a revision number. An index holds copies of those vectors alongside the revision it copied. Queries carry their own vectors plus the set of documents that genuinely resolve them. The gap this chapter lives in comes from separating the index copy from the corpus original. A revised document increments its revision in the corpus and leaves the index untouched, exactly as a real ingest failure would.

Our retrieval model at **app/retrieval.py** comes out like this:

```
"""A small vector index, built so that retrieval quality can be
degraded on purpose."""
from __future__ import annotations

import math
import random
from dataclasses import dataclass, field

DIM = 64
TOPICS = ["settlements", "refunds", "webhooks", "api_errors",
"billing"]


def unit(vector: list[float]) -> list[float]:
    norm = math.sqrt(sum(x * x for x in vector)) or 1.0
    return [x / norm for x in vector]


def dot(a: list[float], b: list[float]) -> float:
    return sum(x * y for x, y in zip(a, b))
```

```
@dataclass
class Document:
    did: int
    topic: str
    vector: list[float]
    revision: int = 0


@dataclass
class Index:
    """What the vector store holds, which may lag the corpus it was
built from."""
    vectors: dict[int, list[float]]
    revisions: dict[int, int]

    @classmethod
    def build(cls, corpus: Corpus) -> "Index":
        return cls(
            {d.did: list(d.vector) for d in
corpus.documents.values()},
            {d.did: d.revision for d in corpus.documents.values()},
        )

    def drop_shard(self, corpus: Corpus, fraction: float, seed: int
= 4) -> None:
        rng = random.Random(seed)
        doomed = [d for d in self.vectors if rng.random() <
fraction]
        for did in doomed:
            self.vectors.pop(did)
            self.revisions.pop(did)

    def search(self, vector: list[float], k: int = 5) ->
list[tuple[int, float]]:
        scored = [(did, dot(vector, vec)) for did, vec in
self.vectors.items()]
        scored.sort(key=lambda pair: pair[1], reverse=True)
        return scored[:k]


def revise_corpus(corpus: Corpus, fraction: float, seed: int = 9) -
> int:
    """Content moves on. The index is not told, so its copies go
stale."""
```

```
    rng = random.Random(seed)
    revised = 0
    for doc in corpus.documents.values():
        if rng.random() < fraction:
            doc.revision += 1
            revised += 1
    return revised
```

The search still returns the document, similarity still scores highly, and the retrieved content is simply wrong. Only recall measured against current revisions rather than against document identity will show it.

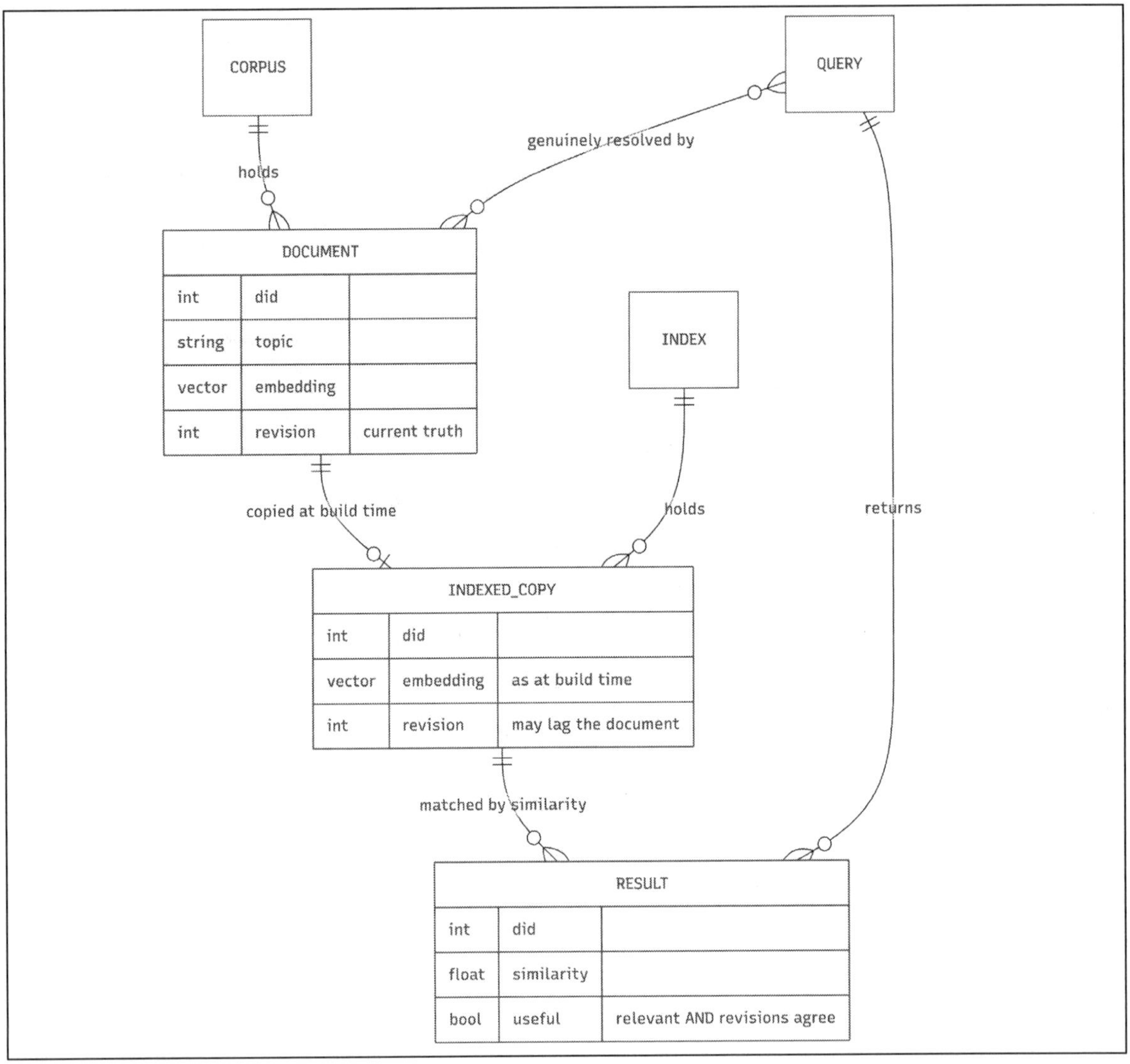

Three Degradations and One Interface

Each failure mode reduces to a single operation against the same objects. The availability degradation calls **drop_shard**, removing a fraction of entries from the index while leaving the corpus intact. The freshness degradation calls **revise_corpus**, incrementing revisions in the corpus while leaving the index intact. Both operate on the gap between the two structures, and they push it in opposite directions.

The compatibility degradation works differently, since it corrupts neither structure. Our **skew_query** helper blends the query vector toward random noise, which reproduces what happens when the ingest embedding model and the query embedding model drift apart. A strength of zero leaves the query untouched, and a strength of one replaces it entirely. No part of the index changes, which matches the real situation where somebody upgrades an embedding service and forgets that eight hundred documents were embedded by its predecessor.

Is Retrieval Helping?

Scoring Against No Retrieval Baseline

Most retrieval evaluation asks how good the retrieval is. A more useful question asks whether retrieval is earning its place, which requires a baseline where the service responds from parametric knowledge alone. Our model therefore carries three probabilities, and only three, with everything else measured from the vectors.

A correct response arrives with probability 0.94 when a current and relevant source reached the prompt. With no retrieval at all, the service resolves 0.62 of the golden set from what the model already knows. The third constant is the interesting one, since a prompt carrying confident but wrong context resolves only 0.38. A bad context is worse than none at all, because it actively displaces what the model would otherwise have said.

The three numbers above are the modelled part of this chapter and we state them plainly rather than burying them. Everything else, including recall, similarity, abstention, and the unsupported rate, comes from real vector arithmetic over eight hundred documents and four hundred queries. A team with production data should replace the three constants with measurements from their own golden set, and every conclusion below will re-derive itself.

That done, here's the scoring harness at **probes/retrieval_probe.py**:

```
# Response model. Only these three constants are assumed;
everything else is measured.
P_GROUNDED = 0.94       # correct when a current, relevant source
reached the prompt
P_MISLED = 0.38         # correct when the prompt carried confident
but wrong context
P_PARAMETRIC = 0.62     # correct with no retrieval at all
```

```
ABSTAIN_BELOW = 0.38    # top similarity under which the service
declines to draft


def evaluate(corpus, index, skew=0.0, abstain_below=ABSTAIN_BELOW,
seed=31) -> Outcome:
    rng = random.Random(seed)
    useful_hits = abstained = unsupported = correct = 0
    similarity_total = 0.0

    for query in corpus.queries:
        vector = skew_query(query.vector, skew) if skew else
query.vector
        results = index.search(vector, 5)
        top1 = results[0][1] if results else 0.0
        similarity_total += top1

        current = corpus.documents
        useful = any(
            did in query.relevant and index.revisions[did] ==
current[did].revision
            for did, _ in results
        )
        useful_hits += int(useful)

        if top1 < abstain_below:
            abstained += 1
            continue
        if useful:
            correct += int(rng.random() < P_GROUNDED)
        else:
            unsupported += 1
            correct += int(rng.random() < P_MISLED)
    ...
```

From this, the harness reports recall, top similarity, abstention, the unsupported rate, and final accuracy for every scenario, which is what lets us compare a degraded configuration against the no retrieval baseline on equal terms. Only the three response probabilities are assumed, and they sit at the top of the file where anybody can replace them with measurements from their own golden set. Everything else in the output comes from vector arithmetic over eight hundred documents and four hundred queries.

Band Where Retrieval Worsens

Every scenario run against the same baseline produces one table that reframes the whole layer.

```
python3 -m probes.retrieval_probe
```

```
no retrieval baseline accuracy is 0.62
scenario                    recall@5  top1sim  abstain   unsupp
accuracy
------------------------------------------------------------------
--------------------------
healthy                       0.9925   0.4969   0.0525    0.005
0.8925  beats no retrieval
shard loss 25%                0.8975   0.4649   0.1725   0.0475
0.7525  beats no retrieval
shard loss 50%                 0.785   0.4322   0.3625   0.0725
0.565  LOSES TO no retrieval
shard loss 80%                0.5625   0.3797    0.615     0.07
0.3225  LOSES TO no retrieval
embedding skew 0.35             0.11   0.3824   0.5025    0.425
0.2575  LOSES TO no retrieval
embedding skew 0.7             0.035   0.3806     0.53     0.45
0.21  LOSES TO no retrieval
index stale 20%               0.9175   0.4969   0.0525   0.0725
0.855  beats no retrieval
index stale 45%                0.765   0.4969   0.0525    0.215
0.765  beats no retrieval
index stale 75%                  0.4   0.4969   0.0525     0.56
0.5775  LOSES TO no retrieval
```

Some five of the nine rows sit below the no retrieval baseline, which is an uncomfortable result and a real one. A service with retrieval switched off entirely would have served users better in every one of those five configurations. None of that conclusion depends on our three constants being exactly right, since the crossover point moves while the existence of a crossover does not.

The two ways of reaching a similar accuracy are worth comparing. A shard loss at fifty percent yields 0.565 with an abstention rate of 36.25 percent, so the service declines more than a third of requests and everyone involved knows something is wrong. Index staleness at seventy five percent yields 0.5775 with an abstention rate of 5.25 percent, identical to a healthy system. Both configurations perform worse than switching retrieval off, and only one of them announces itself.

Similarities and Differences

Abstention Driven by Top Similarity

The single most valuable behaviour a retrieval augmented service can have is abstention, and it needs a trigger. Top similarity is the obvious candidate, since a query that matches nothing well should not produce a confident draft. The threshold takes one calibration sweep against the healthy corpus, because a threshold set too high refuses everything and one set too low refuses nothing.

```
healthy top1 similarity: min 0.329 p05 0.380 median 0.501 max 0.699

threshold sweep, healthy corpus
  0.38: abstain=0.0525 accuracy=0.8925 beats=True
  0.40: abstain=0.095  accuracy=0.8525 beats=True
  0.42: abstain=0.165  accuracy=0.7825 beats=True
  0.44: abstain=0.265  accuracy=0.69   beats=True
  0.46: abstain=0.3425 accuracy=0.615  beats=False
```

Our threshold settles at 0.38, which sits at the fifth percentile of healthy similarity and produces an abstention rate of 5.25 percent. That figure lands inside the refusal envelope we derived at the start, which is a pleasant confirmation that two independently derived numbers agree. A threshold pushed to 0.46 makes the service so cautious that retrieval stops being worthwhile at all.

The same threshold does excellent work on two of the failure modes. A shard loss drives abstention from 5.25 percent to 61.5 percent as the missing documents pull similarity down. An embedding skew drives it past 50 percent, since a query in the wrong space matches nothing convincingly. Both failures become impossible to overlook within minutes, and the service degrades toward silence rather than toward confident nonsense.

Blindness That Matters

Now watch the same threshold against freshness.

```
 stale %  recall@5  top1sim  abstain   unsupp  accuracy  vs no
retrieval
      0%    0.9925   0.4969   0.0525    0.005    0.8925  +0.2725
     20%    0.9175   0.4969   0.0525   0.0725     0.855  +0.2350
     45%     0.765   0.4969   0.0525    0.215     0.765  +0.1450
     60%    0.6175   0.4969   0.0525   0.3575    0.6875  +0.0675
     70%     0.515   0.4969   0.0525   0.4575      0.64  +0.0200
     80%    0.3175   0.4969   0.0525   0.6375      0.54  -0.0800
```

Consider the **top1sim** column closely. Every value is 0.4969, identical to four decimal places at every level of staleness from zero to eighty percent. The abstention holds at 5.25 percent throughout, because the trigger it depends on never moves. Meanwhile the unsupported rate climbs from half a percent to nearly sixty four percent, and accuracy crosses below the no retrieval baseline somewhere between seventy and eighty percent staleness.

Such flatness is not an artefact of our model. The similarity measures the distance between a query vector and a stored vector, and staleness changes neither of them. A stale document matches its query exactly as well as it did on the day it was indexed, because it is the same document with the same embedding. Any abstention mechanism built on similarity is therefore structurally incapable of detecting freshness failure, no matter how carefully the threshold gets tuned.

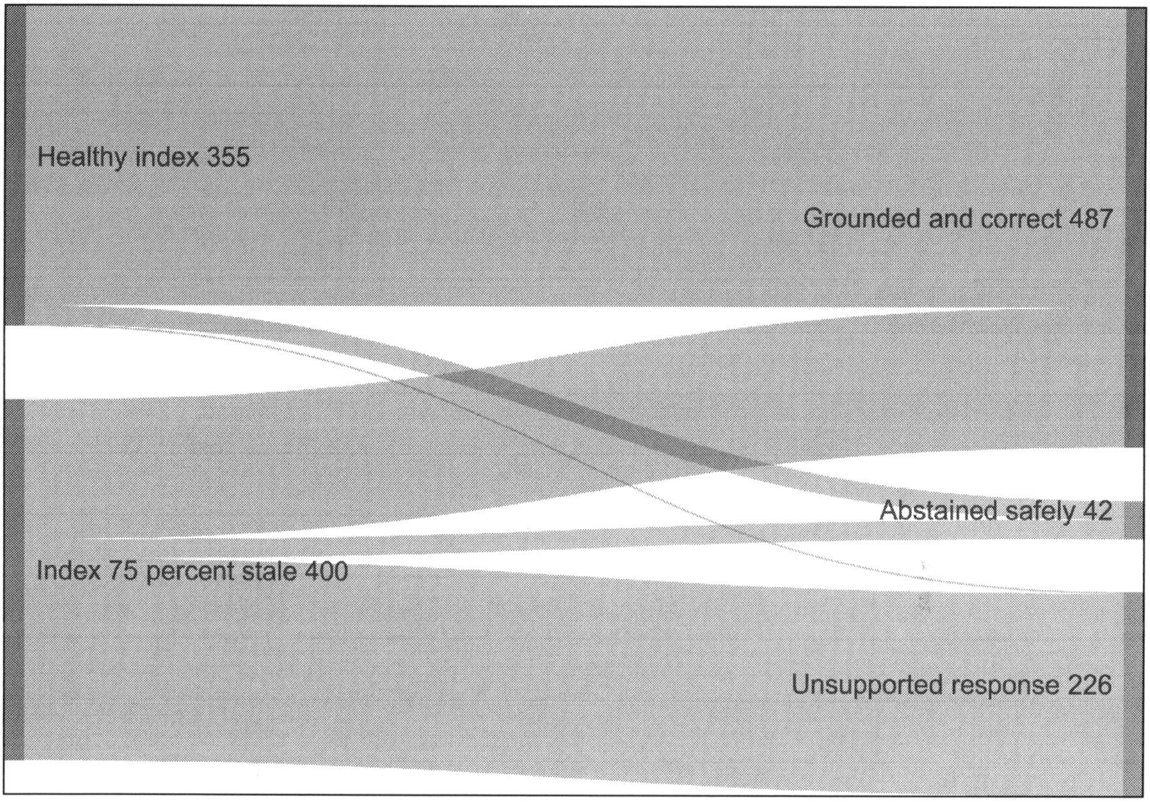

The two available defences have nothing to do with similarity:

1. Our first is an age signal, where the index publishes how long since its last successful full ingest and an envelope caps that at twenty four hours.
2. Our second is a grounding check, where a sampled fraction of responses gets compared against the current source rather than against the retrieved copy.

Both compare the system against something outside itself, which is the only category of check that works here.

Five Experiments and Associated Signals

Committing Two New Signals

Our envelope file gains two entries and rises to schema five. A **`top1_similarity`** floor of 0.46 sits in the retrieval layer, catching availability and compatibility failures. An **`unsupported_rate`** ceiling of 0.025 sits in the boundary layer, catching what actually reaches the user. Our existing **index_age_hours** ceiling of twenty four, declared at the outset and unpopulated ever since, finally gets a measurement behind it.

The layer placement follows the rule Chapter 6 established. The similarity is a property of the retrieval operation, so it belongs to retrieval. An unsupported response is a property of what the support desk received, so it belongs to the boundary. The second signal placed in the retrieval layer would have been defensible and wrong, since it would make every staleness run report itself and the silent classification would evaporate.

Running Scenarios

```
python3 -m probes.retrieval_run --experiment exp-017-index-stale-45
--injection stale-45
```

Our forty five percent staleness run produces the sharpest output in the chapter.

```
signal                      baseline  injection      delta  status
------------------------------------------------------------------
-
golden_set_score              0.8925      0.765    -0.1275  BREACH
index_age_hours                  6.0       96.0       90.0  BREACH
override_rate                 0.0718     0.0718        0.0  inside
recall_at_5                   0.9925      0.765    -0.2275  inside
refusal_rate                  0.0525     0.0525        0.0  inside
top1_similarity               0.4969     0.4969        0.0  inside
ttft_p99_ms                    712.1      712.1        0.0  inside
unsupported_rate               0.005      0.215       0.21  BREACH
------------------------------------------------------------------
-
injection layer : retrieval
breached layers : ['boundary', 'retrieval']
system reported : False
VERDICT         : SILENT
```

The **recall_at_5** entry in that output tells the story. It fell by nearly twenty three points and still sits inside its floor of 0.733, so the signal most teams would reach for first missed the fault entirely. The similarity did not move by a thousandth. Only three signals fired, and two of them exist because we wrote them down speculatively at the outset, before anybody knew how to measure them.

Our shard loss run at twenty five percent produced a related surprise. The similarity fell to 0.4649, which sits just above the 0.46 floor and therefore held. Every breach in that run landed in the boundary layer instead, driven by an abstention rate of 17.25 percent and an unsupported rate of 4.75 percent. An availability failure announces itself through user facing signals well before the retrieval layer's own signal notices anything.

Recording Findings

Fault	Tool	Signal watched	Verdict	Finding
Retrieval latency plus 200ms	Chaos Mesh NetworkChaos	ttft_p99_ms, recall_at_5	Absorbed	Nothing breached, retrieval has adequate latency headroom at this arrival rate
Vector store replica killed, 25 percent shard loss	Chaos Mesh PodChaos	top1_similarity, refusal_rate, unsupported_rate	Cascaded	Similarity held at 0.4649 just above its floor; abstention tripled and caught it instead
Embedding skew of 0.35 between ingest and query	Config change	recall_at_5, top1_similarity, refusal_rate	Cascaded	Recall collapsed to 0.11 and half of all requests were declined, impossible to overlook
Index 45 percent stale, 96 hours since ingest	Config change	index_age_hours, unsupported_rate, golden_set_score	Silent	Similarity unchanged to four decimal places, recall inside its floor, 21.5 percent unsupported
Index 75 percent stale, 168 hours since ingest	Config change	index_age_hours, unsupported_rate, golden_set_score	Silent	Accuracy fell below the no retrieval baseline while abstention held at exactly 5.25 percent

No degraded verdict appears in that table, and its absence is a finding rather than an omission. Our retrieval layer has no channel through which to report its own trouble, so every fault here either vanished into the system's tolerance or reached the boundary layer before anything reacted. In Chapter 8 we move to that boundary directly, where we begin injecting faults into the responses themselves.

Summary

We built an index whose copies can lag the corpus they came from, which made freshness failure expressible rather than merely describable. Every degradation scored against a no retrieval baseline then produced the uncomfortable result that five of nine configurations performed worse than switching retrieval off. A bad context displaces what the model would otherwise have said, so a broken retrieval layer costs more than an absent one.

Our similarity based abstention handled availability and compatibility failures well, driving refusals from five percent to over sixty as documents vanished or queries landed in the wrong space. Faced with staleness it did nothing at all, since top similarity held at 0.4969 across every level from zero to eighty percent while unsupported responses climbed to sixty four percent. A pair of new signals now covers that blindness, and our verdict rules revealed that retrieval can never produce a degraded result. In Chapter 8 we move to the model boundary.

CHAPTER 8
MODEL-BOUNDARY CHAOS

In Chapter 7 we ended with a retrieval layer that has no voice, where every fault either vanished into tolerance or reached the user before anything complained. Our vector store behaved perfectly throughout, returning exactly what it was asked for. We now cross the last boundary before the user, into the response itself, where the same pattern repeats with sharper consequences.

Across this chapter, we will build a fault library as pure functions, wrap it in a mitmproxy addon, and drive nine distinct faults through a live proxy against a real agent. Our matrix measures four outcomes per fault, namely whether the agent detected it, whether the task succeeded, whether a wrong action was executed, and whether the prose reaching the user was cut short. Exactly three faults produce zero detection. A single one of them makes the agent execute a real lookup against the wrong record and report the result with complete confidence.

Fault Class between Network and Model

Why Neither Kubernetes Tool Can Reach?

We settled on three tools when the lab was built, and gave each a clear boundary. The orchestration falls to LitmusChaos, Chaos Mesh reaches the kernel and the filesystem, and mitmproxy handles what neither can touch. Seven chapters later we finally need the third, because every fault so far has been expressible as a change to infrastructure state.

Consider what Chaos Mesh can do to a model response. A network delay slows the bytes, packet loss breaks the connection, and partition prevents the call entirely. All three operate on the transport, so all three produce failures a caller recognises immediately. None of them can alter a single field inside a well formed payload, because the transport has no interest in what the bytes mean. Our dangerous faults live entirely in that meaning. A response arrives with a two hundred status, correct content length, valid JSON, and a tool call whose arguments point at the wrong account. Every layer beneath the application sees a perfect transaction. That fault requires something that parses the payload, changes it, and re-serialises it, which is precisely what an intercepting proxy does.

Taxonomy Worth Building Against

Our nine faults cover the space adequately, and grouping them by what they break makes the pattern visible before we run anything. A transport fault breaks the connection or the status, so **`drop`** and **`rate_limit`** belong here. A structural fault leaves the transport intact and makes the payload unparseable, covering **`malformed_json`** and **`truncate_open`**. A contract fault produces valid JSON that violates the agreed shape, which is what **`schema_violation`** does by renaming a required field.

The two further groups matter more than the first three combined. A semantic fault produces valid JSON satisfying every contract while carrying wrong values, which is **`bad_tool_args`**. A completeness fault produces valid, contract satisfying, semantically correct output that simply stops early and closes cleanly, which is **`truncate_clean`**. Our ninth fault, **`fallback_model`**, substitutes a weaker model's reply and belongs in a category of its own.

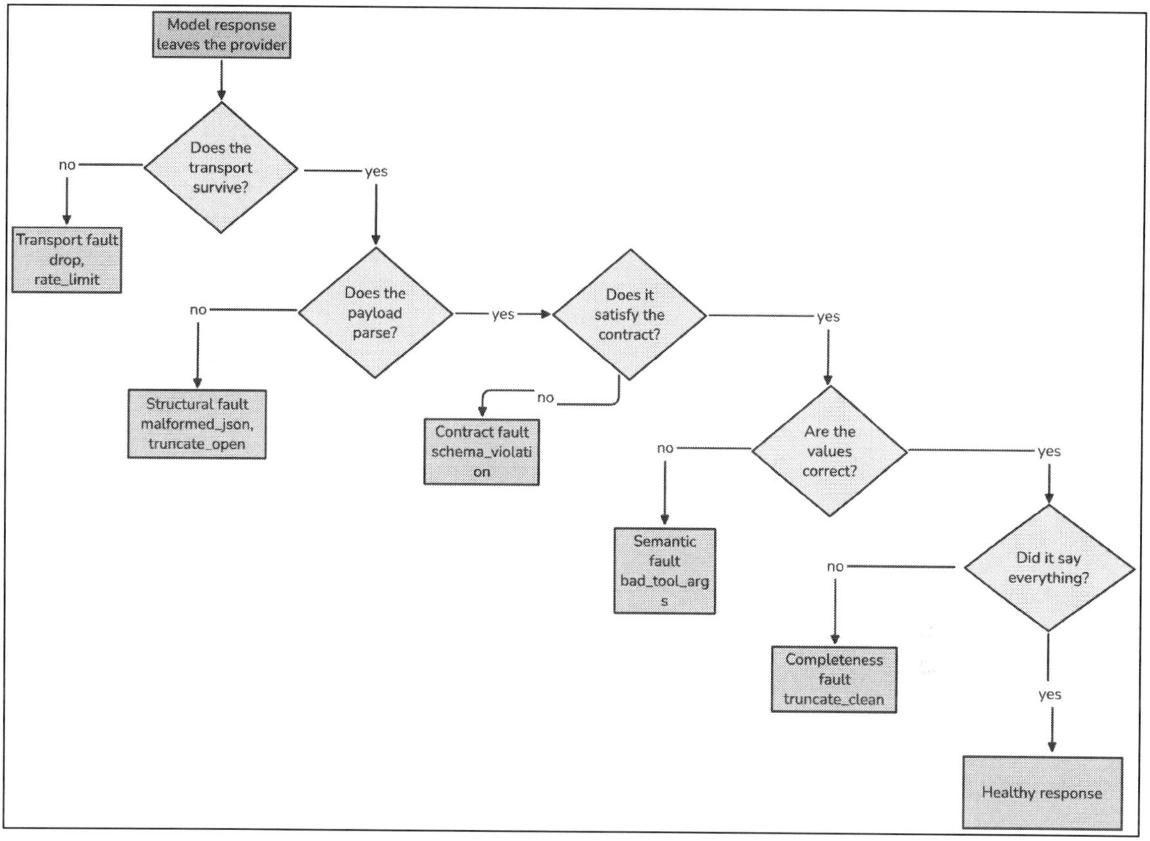

That flow read from top to bottom yields a prediction. Each level down leaves more of the system's defences intact, so detection should get harder as we descend. A transport fault trips an exception handler, a structural fault trips a parser, and a contract fault trips a validator. Below that line nothing in a conventional stack is watching, since a semantically wrong response satisfies every check anybody wrote.

Building Injection Point

Faults as Pure Functions

Our fault library takes and returns a triple of status, headers, and body. A signature that plain means the same functions run inside the proxy, inside a unit test, and inside any replay tool we build later. No part of the library imports mitmproxy, so testing it needs no proxy at all.

So, here's what the fault library at **`app/boundary_faults.py`** holds:

```
"""Faults applied to a model response after it is generated and
before it is used.

Every function takes and returns a (status, headers, body) triple,
so the same
code runs inside a mitmproxy addon, inside a unit test, or inside a
replay tool.
"""
from __future__ import annotations

import json
import random
from typing import Callable

Triple = tuple[int, dict[str, str], bytes]
JSON_CT = {"content-type": "application/json"}


def truncate_clean(status: int, headers: dict[str, str], body:
bytes, rng: random.Random) -> Triple:
    """Content shortened, then closed properly. Parses, and says
less than it should."""
    payload = json.loads(body)
    message = payload["choices"][0]["message"]
    if message.get("content"):
        words = message["content"].split()
        message["content"] = " ".join(words[: max(3, len(words) //
3)])
    payload["choices"][0]["finish_reason"] = "stop"
    return status, headers, json.dumps(payload).encode()


def schema_violation(status: int, headers: dict[str, str], body:
bytes, rng: random.Random) -> Triple:
    """Valid JSON, renamed required field. Structurally fine,
contractually broken."""
    payload = json.loads(body)
    calls = payload["choices"][0]["message"].get("tool_calls")
    if calls:
        calls[0]["function"]["arguments_json"] =
calls[0]["function"].pop("arguments")
    return status, headers, json.dumps(payload).encode()


def bad_tool_args(status: int, headers: dict[str, str], body:
```

```
bytes, rng: random.Random) -> Triple:
    """Valid JSON, valid schema, wrong values. Nothing downstream
can tell."""
    payload = json.loads(body)
    calls = payload["choices"][0]["message"].get("tool_calls")
    if calls:
        args = json.loads(calls[0]["function"]["arguments"])
        if "settlement_id" in args:
            digits = "".join(ch for ch in
str(args["settlement_id"]) if ch.isdigit())
            shifted = str(int(digits or "0") + 1).zfill(len(digits)
or 1)
            args["settlement_id"] =
str(args["settlement_id"]).replace(digits, shifted)
        calls[0]["function"]["arguments"] = json.dumps(args)
    return status, headers, json.dumps(payload).encode()


def fallback_model(status: int, headers: dict[str, str], body:
bytes, rng: random.Random) -> Triple:
    """Primary unavailable, weaker model answered. Same shape, less
capability."""
    payload = json.loads(body)
    payload["model"] = "helpmate-fallback-3b"
    message = payload["choices"][0]["message"]
    message.pop("tool_calls", None)
    message["content"] = (
        "I am not able to look that up right now. Settlements
usually clear "
        "within two business days."
    )
    return status, headers, json.dumps(payload).encode()
```

The **`bad_tool_args`** function deserves a close look, since the subtlety is the point. The settlement identifier **`STL-90210`** becomes **`STL-90211`**, a single digit apart and entirely valid. Our ledger holds both, where the first cleared at 4,182.60 and settled, while the second reversed at 17,940.00. Any agent acting on that argument performs a genuine lookup, receives a genuine record, and reports a figure four times too large with the wrong status attached.

'mitmproxy' Addon and Its Control File

Our addon does very little, which is the correct amount. The active fault comes from a control file on every response rather than from an environment variable, which means the whole matrix runs against one long lived proxy. A restart of mitmproxy nine times over would work and would take a minute of waiting per fault.

Here's what we can now write in the addon at **probes/mitm_boundary.py**:

```
"""mitmproxy addon that applies one boundary fault to every model
response.

The active fault is read from a control file on each response, so
the matrix
can be driven without restarting the proxy.
"""
from __future__ import annotations

import logging
import os
import random
from pathlib import Path

from mitmproxy import http

from app.boundary_faults import FAULTS, apply

CONTROL = Path(os.environ.get("BOUNDARY_CONTROL", "results/current-
fault"))
RNG = random.Random(int(os.environ.get("BOUNDARY_SEED", "17")))


def active_fault() -> tuple[str, float]:
    if not CONTROL.exists():
        return "none", 1.0
    parts = CONTROL.read_text(encoding="utf-8").split()
    name = parts[0] if parts else "none"
    rate = float(parts[1]) if len(parts) > 1 else 1.0
    return (name if name in FAULTS else "none"), rate


def response(flow: http.HTTPFlow) -> None:
    fault, rate = active_fault()
    if fault == "none" or RNG.random() > rate:
        return
    headers = {k.lower(): v for k, v in
flow.response.headers.items()}
    status, new_headers, body = apply(
        fault, flow.response.status_code, flow.response.content,
RNG
    )
    flow.response = http.Response.make(status, body, new_headers)
```

```
    logging.info(f"boundary fault {fault} applied to
{flow.request.path}")
```

The reverse proxy mode keeps the agent unchanged, since the agent simply points at a different port. No part of HelpMate needs to know a proxy exists, which matters because a fault injection technique requiring application changes will never be trusted near production.

The upstream and the proxy in front of it start like this:

```
python3 -m app.model_api &
PYTHONPATH=$PWD mitmdump \
  --mode reverse:http://127.0.0.1:9200 \
  --listen-host 127.0.0.1 --listen-port 9300 \
  -s probes/mitm_boundary.py -q &
```

An empty control file means passthrough, so the first thing to confirm is that a request through port 8081 returns exactly what port 9200 returns. Once that holds, switching faults is a single write to the control file rather than a restart, which is what keeps the nine fault matrix down to a few seconds per row.

Something to Break

Upstream that Speaks Chat Completion Shape

Our stand in provider returns a tool call rather than prose, because tool calls are where semantic faults do real damage. The two settlements in its ledger sit deliberately one digit apart, and the difference between them is the difference between a routine confirmation and a serious error.

Our next task is the upstream at **app/model_api.py**, and here's what it contains:

```
LEDGER = {
    "STL-90210": {"account": "ACC-4417", "amount": "4,182.60",
"status": "settled"},
    "STL-90211": {"account": "ACC-4417", "amount": "17,940.00",
"status": "reversed"},
}


def completion(settlement_id: str) -> dict:
    return {
        "id": "cmpl-8841",
        "model": "helpmate-8b",
        "choices": [
            {
                "index": 0,
```

```
                "finish_reason": "tool_calls",
                "message": {
                    "role": "assistant",
                    "content": (
                        "I will look up that settlement and confirm
the cleared "
                        "amount along with its current status for
you."
                    ),
                    "tool_calls": [
                        {
                            "id": "call_1",
                            "type": "function",
                            "function": {
                                "name": "lookup_settlement",
                                "arguments": json.dumps(
                                    {"account_id": "ACC-4417",
"settlement_id": settlement_id}
                                ),
                            },
                        }
                    ],
                },
            }
        ],
    }
```

The ledger is the part that makes this upstream worth building rather than mocking. Both settlements exist, so an agent that receives **STL-90211** in place of **STL-90210** performs a genuine lookup, receives a genuine record, and reports a reversed payment of 17,940.00 with complete confidence. A fault that returns nonsense would be caught by any validator, and a fault that returns a real record belonging to somebody else will not be.

Agent that Acts on Response

Our agent behaves the way most production agents behave, which is to say it defends against the failures it has seen before. Non-success statuses trigger a retry, unparseable payloads trigger a retry, and a missing **arguments** field fails schema validation. Beyond that it trusts what it received, because nothing in the response suggests distrust is warranted. Against that background we record four outcomes per attempt. The first captures whether the agent noticed anything wrong. The second captures whether the support desk received the correct settlement detail. The third captures whether the agent executed a real lookup against a record it should never have touched. The fourth captures whether the prose shown to the user was cut short.

For now, we can write the agent at **app/agent_client.py** like this:

```
def run(endpoint: str, timeout: float = 4.0) -> Attempt:
    attempt = Attempt()
    started = time.perf_counter()

    for _ in range(MAX_RETRIES + 1):
        status, body = call_once(endpoint, timeout)
        if status != 200:
            attempt.detected = True
            attempt.failure = f"http {status}"
            attempt.retries += 1
            continue
        try:
            payload = json.loads(body)
        except json.JSONDecodeError:
            attempt.detected = True
            attempt.failure = "unparseable body"
            attempt.retries += 1
            continue

        message = payload.get("choices", [{}])[0].get("message",
{})
        calls = message.get("tool_calls")
        if not calls:
            attempt.content_complete = len(message.get("content",
"").split()) >= NOMINAL_WORDS * 0.6
            attempt.failure = "no tool call offered"
            attempt.seconds = time.perf_counter() - started
            return attempt
        function = calls[0].get("function", {})
        if "arguments" not in function:
            attempt.detected = True
            attempt.failure = "tool call failed schema validation"
            attempt.seconds = time.perf_counter() - started
            return attempt

        prose = message.get("content", "")
        attempt.content_complete = len(prose.split()) >=
NOMINAL_WORDS * 0.6

        args = json.loads(function["arguments"])
        record = LEDGER.get(args.get("settlement_id"))
        attempt.acted_wrongly = args.get("settlement_id") !=
TRUTH["settlement_id"]
        if record and record["amount"] == TRUTH["amount"]:
            attempt.succeeded = True
```

```
    else:
        attempt.failure = "reported the wrong settlement"
    attempt.seconds = time.perf_counter() - started
    return attempt
```

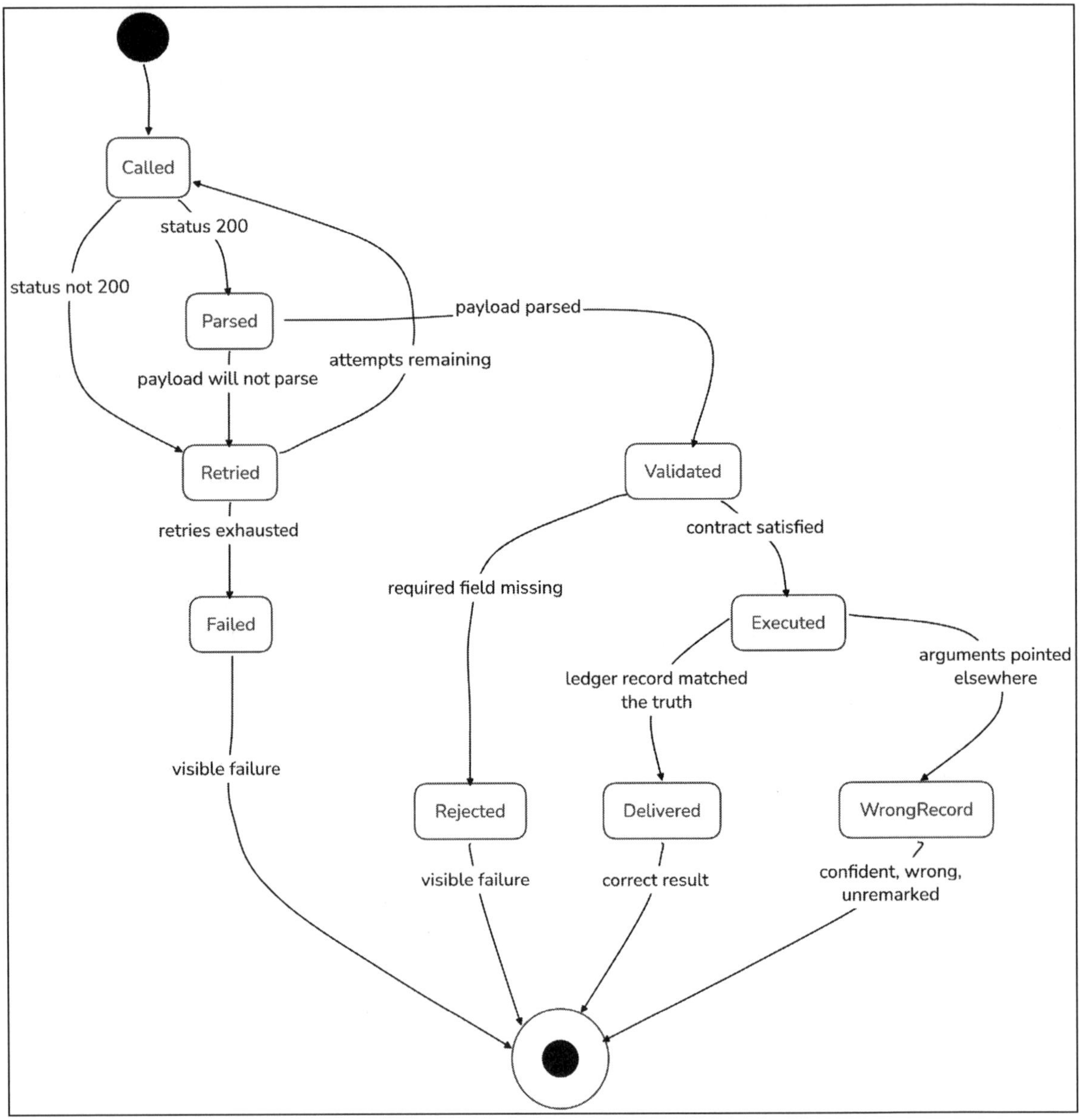

Fault Matrix

Running Faults through Live Proxy

A run of sixty trials per fault against the live proxy takes a few seconds and produces the table this chapter exists for.

```
python3 -m probes.boundary_matrix --trials 60
```

fault	detected	succeeded	wrong action	content cut	retries	seconds
none	0.0	1.0	0.0	0.0	0.0	0.004
drop	1.0	0.0	0.0	0.0	3.0	0.01
rate_limit	1.0	0.0	0.0	0.0	3.0	0.01
malformed_json	1.0	0.0	0.0	0.0	3.0	0.01
truncate_open	1.0	0.0	0.0	0.0	3.0	0.01
truncate_clean	0.0	1.0	0.0	1.0	0.0	0.003
schema_violation	1.0	0.0	0.0	0.0	0.0	0.003
bad_tool_args	0.0	0.0	1.0	0.0	0.0	0.003
fallback_model	0.0	0.0	0.0	0.0	0.0	0.003

Our prediction from the taxonomy holds exactly. The transport and structural faults reach a detection rate of one and burn three retries each, so a caller under those conditions triples its load on an already failing provider. The contract faults reach detection without retries, since a schema failure is not worth retrying. Below the contract line, detection falls to zero and stays there.

Control Run that Proves Proxy Did

We need one more run before attributing those differences to the proxy. The same matrix pointed straight at the upstream, with mitmproxy bypassed entirely, should produce nine identical healthy rows.

```
python3 -m probes.boundary_matrix \
  --endpoint http://127.0.0.1:9200/v1/chat/completions --trials 20
```

fault	detected	succeeded	wrong action	content cut	retries	seconds
none	0.0	1.0	0.0	0.0	0.0	0.001
drop	0.0	1.0	0.0	0.0	0.0	0.001
rate_limit	0.0	1.0	0.0	0.0	0.0	0.0
malformed_json	0.0	1.0	0.0	0.0	0.0	0.0
truncate_open	0.0	1.0	0.0	0.0	0.0	0.0
truncate_clean	0.0	1.0	0.0	0.0	0.0	0.0
schema_violation	0.0	1.0	0.0	0.0	0.0	0.0
bad_tool_args	0.0	1.0	0.0	0.0	0.0	0.0
fallback_model	0.0	1.0	0.0	0.0	0.0	0.0

Every row succeeds, which establishes that the entire effect comes from the injection layer rather than from anything in the agent or the upstream. A control like that costs twenty seconds and settles an argument that would otherwise consume an afternoon. Any experiment whose result cannot be switched off is an observation rather than an experiment.

Three Faults with Zero Detection

The three rows carrying a detection rate of zero fail in three different ways. Our **`truncate_clean`** row succeeds at the task while cutting the prose to a third of its length, so the support agent receives a correct settlement figure wrapped in a sentence that stops mid thought. The damage there is modest and the pattern matters, since the same fault applied to a response with no tool call removes information nobody knows is missing.

Our **`fallback_model`** row neither succeeds nor acts wrongly. A weaker model returned a plausible, polite, entirely useless reply about settlements generally clearing within two business days. No part of that response is malformed, nothing violates a schema, and the agent has no basis for objecting. The failover worked exactly as designed and the user received nothing of value.

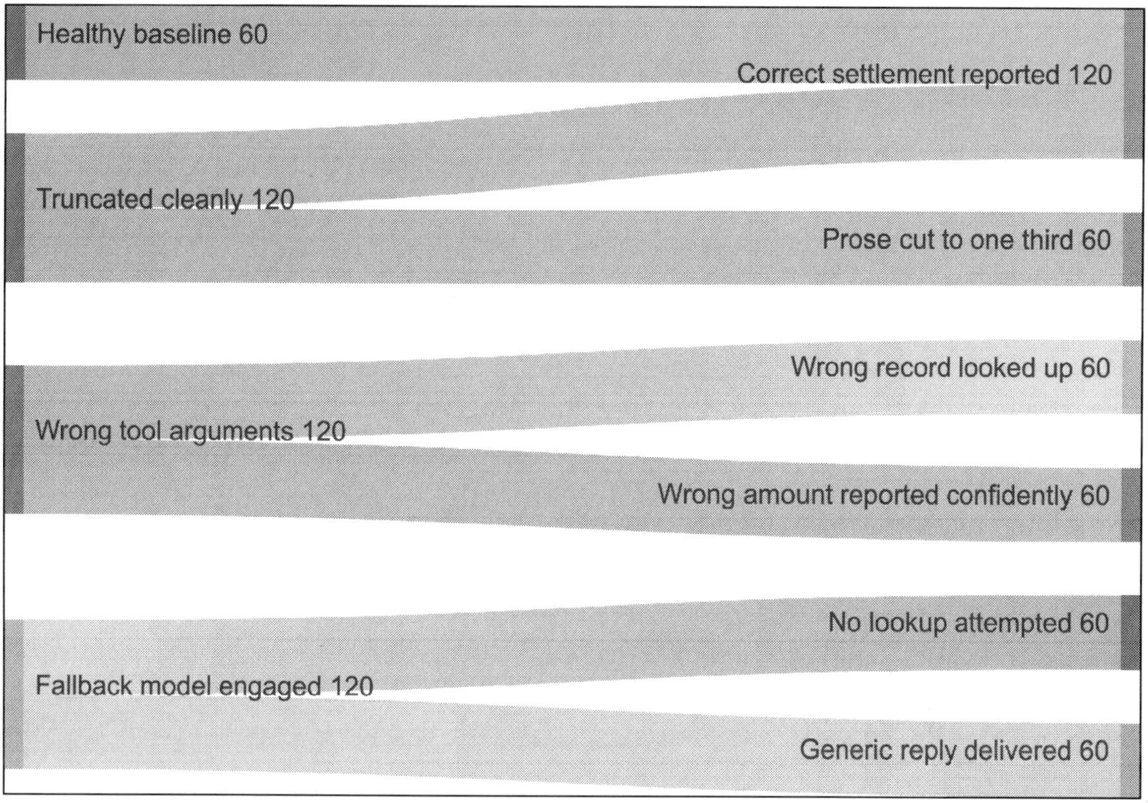

Our **`bad_tool_args`** row is the one to take to a design review. The agent received a valid response, validated it successfully, executed a genuine ledger lookup, and reported that settlement STL-90211 had reversed for 17,940.00. Every step in that sequence worked. A support agent reading the draft has no reason to doubt it, since the figure is specific, the status is definite, and the identifier is one character from the one they asked about.

Signals, Verdicts and Findings

Two New Agent Signals and Distress Rule

The agent layer gains two signals, and one long declared signal finally gets a measurement. Our **`wrong_action_rate`** carries a ceiling of zero, because there is no acceptable rate at which an agent executes real actions on wrong arguments. Our **`retry_amplification`** carries a ceiling of 0.2 retries per request, which catches the storms transport faults produce. We declared **`response_validity`** with a floor of 0.90 at the outset and nothing ever populated it, and the matrix supplies it now as one minus the detection rate.

A rule in our verdict logic needs extending, and the extension is worth explaining rather than slipping in. Our distress signals were **`refusal_rate`** and **`escalation_rate`**, both representing the system openly admitting it cannot cope. The boundary faults produce two further admissions of the same kind. A collapsing **`response_validity`** means the agent is rejecting responses out loud, and a rising **`retry_amplification`** means it is visibly struggling. Both additions keep the loud faults classified as loud. The change matters less than the verification of it, since the verdict rules now decide every result in the book. Our four branch coverage test runs unchanged and still passes, which confirms the extension did not disturb the existing classifications. We re-ran the regressions across Chapters 2 through 7 for the same reason.

Recording Findings

Fault	Tool	Signal watched	Verdict	Finding
No fault, proxy in the path	mitmproxy	all boundary and agent signals	Absorbed	The proxy itself costs nothing measurable, one millisecond on average
Response dropped, 502 returned	mitmproxy	response_validity, retry_amplification	Cascaded	Detected every time, three retries per request, load tripled on a failing provider
Required field renamed in the tool call	mitmproxy	response_validity, tool_call_success	Cascaded	Schema validation caught all sixty, no retries wasted, failure visible immediately
Content cut to one third, stream closed cleanly	mitmproxy	truncated_valid_rate	Silent	Task succeeded, every response reached the user missing two thirds of its prose
Tool arguments shifted by one digit	mitmproxy	wrong_action_rate	Silent	Sixty genuine lookups against the wrong record, 17,940.00 reversed reported instead of 4,182.60 settled
Weaker fallback model substituted	mitmproxy	tool_call_success	Silent	No lookup attempted, generic reply delivered, failover reported as a success everywhere

Our three silent rows from six experiments make the highest proportion in the book so far, and the layer explains why. Every defence our agent carries was written against a failure somebody had already met, so transport, parsing, and schema all have handlers. No defence anybody wrote covers a response that is correct in every respect except the one that matters.

Summary

We finally used the third tool, seven chapters after choosing it. Our nine faults grouped into five categories predicted that detection would fall as each layer of defence was left intact, and a live matrix through mitmproxy confirmed the prediction exactly. The transport and structural faults were caught every time at the cost of three retries each. The contract faults were caught without retries. Below the contract line, detection reached zero and stayed there.

Our worst result involved a settlement identifier shifted by one digit. The agent validated the response, executed a real ledger lookup, and reported a reversed payment of 17,940.00 in place of a settled 4,182.60, sixty times out of sixty, with no signal anywhere. A control run with the proxy bypassed produced nine clean rows, which proves the effect belongs to the injection rather than to the harness. In Chapter 9 we follow the agent past the boundary into the actions it takes.

CHAPTER 9
AGENTIC AND MULTI-AGENT CHAOS

In Chapter 8 we ended with an agent that validated a response, executed a genuine ledger lookup, and reported a reversed payment of 17,940.00 in place of a settled 4,182.60. Every defence it carried worked exactly as written. We now follow that agent past the boundary into the actions it takes, and into the pipelines where its output becomes somebody else's input.

Across this chapter, we will trace a single wrong fact through three pipeline stages and measure how much damage arrives at the far end. Our attention then turns to the reframing this book has been building toward, namely that every autonomous action touching infrastructure is itself a fault event. We will build a remediation agent, watch it make things worse, then build the gate that stops it. The envelope file gains two new signals, and an action ledger puts agent decisions in the same record as our injected faults.

Agent Breaks Two Ways

Agent as Victim

Our first frame is the familiar one, where the agent receives something bad and copes badly. In Chapter 8 we covered the single call case thoroughly, and pipelines change the arithmetic. A degraded output at stage one becomes the input at stage two, which produces several outputs of its own, each inheriting the original error and adding a little.

That kind of compounding is not additive, and the difference matters for how we set thresholds. A pipeline where each stage derives two facts from each fact it receives will double the population at every hop. A single wrong fact entering the first stage therefore has two chances to reproduce, then four, and a corrective step at stage three has to catch a majority rather than a minority. Most teams size their review effort against the fault they injected rather than against the fault that arrives. The recovery behaves oddly too. Later stages frequently do a competent job of processing wrong input, producing a fluent and internally consistent draft built on a false premise. Our quality signals measured at the final stage look reasonable, since the prose is well formed and the tone is right. No part of the output reveals that its foundation was laid incorrectly two stages earlier.

Agent as Injector

Our second frame is the one almost nobody applies. When a remediation agent restarts a service, scales a deployment, reroutes traffic, or edits a configuration, it has injected a fault into a running system. No property distinguishes that action from an experiment except our intent and the absence of a controlled window.

Consider what a human on call does before restarting anything during an incident. They check how much error budget remains this month. They look at whether a shared dependency is already saturated. They ask whether a deploy went out recently, because a restart during a rollout compounds two changes. Finally they check whether anybody is around to watch. Every one of those checks is a judgement about whether the system can absorb additional stress right now. An autonomous agent skips all four. It observes an anomaly, selects an action from its policy, and executes. Such behaviour is not a defect in the agent, since nothing in its design ever asked those questions. Our chaos programme has spent chapters building the exact signals a human would consult, and the agent is not connected to any of them. That gap is the practical work of this chapter.

Tracing Damage across Pipeline

Facts as Travelling Unit

Any measurement of propagation needs something countable moving between stages. Our pipeline therefore passes facts rather than prose, where each fact carries an identifier, the stage that produced it, whether it is correct, and which fact it descended from. That parentage is what makes tracing possible, since a wrong fact at the draft stage can be walked back to its origin. Our pipeline runs that work across three stages. The triage stage extracts six facts from a ticket. The enrichment stage derives two further facts from each one, so a wrong parent tends to produce wrong children. The drafting stage then selects three of those as critical, and the run succeeds only when all three critical facts survive. Every stage adds its own small error rate on top of what it inherited.

We now write the pipeline at **app/pipeline.py** as below:

```
"""A three stage agent pipeline, built so that damage can be traced
across stages.

Facts are the unit that travels. Stage one extracts them from a
ticket, stage two
derives further facts from each one, and stage three drafts from
everything it has.
"""
from __future__ import annotations

import random
from dataclasses import dataclass, field

STAGES = ("triage", "enrich", "draft")
CRITICAL = 3            # facts the final draft must get right to be
correct


@dataclass
class Fact:
    fid: str
    stage: str
    correct: bool
```

```
    parent: str | None = None
    critical: bool = False


@dataclass
class Run:
    facts: list[Fact] = field(default_factory=list)
    injected: int = 0

    def wrong_at(self, stage: str) -> int:
        return sum(1 for f in self.facts if f.stage == stage and
not f.correct)

    def cascade_depth(self) -> int:
        """How many stages carry at least one wrong fact."""
        return sum(1 for stage in STAGES if self.wrong_at(stage) >
0)

    def succeeded(self) -> bool:
        critical = [f for f in self.facts if f.stage == "draft" and
f.critical]
        return bool(critical) and all(f.correct for f in critical)


def run_pipeline(
    rng: random.Random,
    triage_facts: int = 6,
    injected_wrong: int = 0,
    stage_error: float = 0.015,
    inherit: float = 0.90,
    fanout: int = 2,
) -> Run:
    run = Run(injected=injected_wrong)

    for index in range(triage_facts):
        forced_wrong = index < injected_wrong
        correct = False if forced_wrong else rng.random() >
stage_error
        run.facts.append(Fact(f"t{index}", "triage", correct))

    for parent in run.by_stage("triage"):
        for child in range(fanout):
            if not parent.correct:
                correct = rng.random() > inherit
            else:
                correct = rng.random() > stage_error
```

```
            run.facts.append(
                Fact(f"{parent.fid}e{child}", "enrich", correct,
parent=parent.fid)
            )
    ...
```

Every fact the pipeline emits carries the stage that produced it and the fact it descended from, which is what turns amplification from an intuition into a number we can count. Our run is deterministic under a fixed seed, so a scenario can be repeated exactly and a surprising result can be inspected rather than argued about. What the next section injects is a single wrong fact at triage, and what it measures is how many wrong facts arrive at the draft.

One Wrong Fact at Stage One

A sweep of the injected fact count across four hundred runs each produces the shape of the compounding.

```
python3 -m probes.cascade_sweep --runs 400
```

injected	wrong triage	wrong enrich	wrong draft	depth	success	amplified
0	0.09	0.33	0.47	0.66	0.897	-
1	1.07	2.07	2.16	2.99	0.530	2.01x
2	2.06	3.81	3.88	3.00	0.318	1.89x
3	3.04	5.59	5.61	3.00	0.107	1.84x
4	4.03	7.33	7.29	3.00	0.015	1.81x
5	5.01	9.11	9.02	3.00	0.005	1.80x
6	6.00	10.85	10.72	3.00	0.000	1.79x

The first two rows read against each other carry the whole finding. A healthy pipeline succeeds 89.7 percent of the time and carries wrong facts in two thirds of one stage on average. A single wrong fact injected at triage drops success to 53.0 percent, which is a fall of nearly thirty seven points from one bad extraction. The cascade depth jumps from 0.66 to 2.99, meaning almost every run now carries corruption in all three stages.

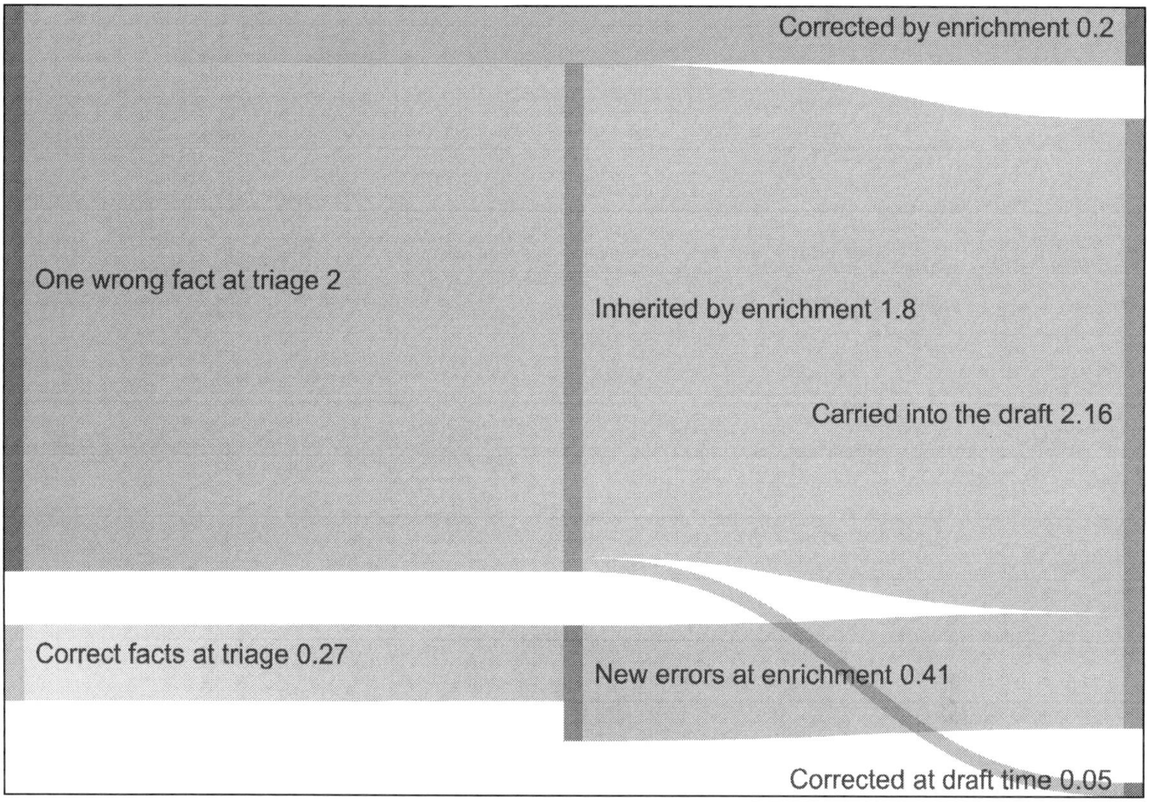

The amplification runs at roughly two for every injection level tested. A single wrong fact at triage becomes 2.16 wrong facts at the draft, and three become 5.61. A review process sized against the original error will catch half of what actually needs catching. With three wrong facts at stage one, which is half of the triage output, the pipeline succeeds only 10.7 percent of the time.

Agent Actions are Chaos Events

Agent Skips Human Judgement

Our remediation agent watches one signal and owns one policy. A latency above the envelope means scale up, and latency far above the envelope means restart. No part of that policy is unreasonable, and versions of it run in production at a great many organisations today.

A human faces four checks before the same action. Our error budget check refuses when less than thirty percent of the monthly budget remains, on the grounds that a system already consuming its reliability headroom should not receive more stress. Our saturation check refuses when the busiest shared dependency sits above eighty percent, because a restart drives a thundering herd into whatever is already struggling. Our deploy recency check refuses within thirty minutes of a rollout, since compounding two changes makes attribution impossible afterwards.

Our fourth check has nothing to do with system state. Somebody has to be watching. An agent acting at three in the morning on a holiday weekend, with nobody available to notice the consequence, is taking a risk nobody consented to. A presence check encoded as a gate condition sounds bureaucratic until the first time an unattended action turns a degradation into an outage.

Building Gate

The decision and the permission stay testable when kept apart. Our **choose** function produces what the agent wants based on the anomaly alone. Our **gate** function then applies the four checks and either passes the decision through or converts it into an escalation.

Both live at **app/remediation.py**, written like this:

```
"""An autonomous remediation agent, and the gate that decides
whether it may act."""
from __future__ import annotations

from dataclasses import dataclass

ACTIONS = ("wait", "restart", "scale_up", "escalate")


@dataclass
class Observation:
    ttft_p99_ms: float
    error_budget_left: float        # fraction of the monthly budget
remaining
    pool_saturation: float          # busiest shared dependency, 0 to
1
    minutes_since_deploy: int
    operator_watching: bool


@dataclass
class Decision:
    action: str
    reason: str
    gated: bool = False


def choose(observation: Observation, ttft_ceiling: float) ->
Decision:
    """What the agent wants to do, judged only on the anomaly it
can see."""
    if observation.ttft_p99_ms > ttft_ceiling * 1.5:
        return Decision("restart", "latency far above ceiling")
```

```
    if observation.ttft_p99_ms > ttft_ceiling:
        return Decision("scale_up", "latency above ceiling")
    return Decision("wait", "inside the envelope")


def gate(decision: Decision, observation: Observation, floor: float
= 0.30) -> Decision:
    """The checks a human on call would run before touching
anything."""
    if decision.action in ("wait", "escalate"):
        return decision
    if observation.error_budget_left < floor:
        return Decision("escalate", f"error budget at
{observation.error_budget_left:.2f}", True)
    if observation.pool_saturation > 0.80:
        return Decision("escalate", f"shared pool at
{observation.pool_saturation:.2f}", True)
    if observation.minutes_since_deploy < 30:
        return Decision("escalate", f"deploy
{observation.minutes_since_deploy} minutes ago", True)
    if not observation.operator_watching:
        return Decision("escalate", "no named operator watching",
True)
    return decision
```

Each check exercised independently confirms all four fire for the right reason.

```
agent wants  : restart    because latency far above ceiling
gate returns : escalate   because error budget at 0.18 (gated=True)
  budget healthy  -> restart    latency far above ceiling
  pool saturated  -> escalate   shared pool at 0.92
  recent deploy   -> escalate   deploy 12 minutes ago
  nobody watching -> escalate   no named operator watching
```

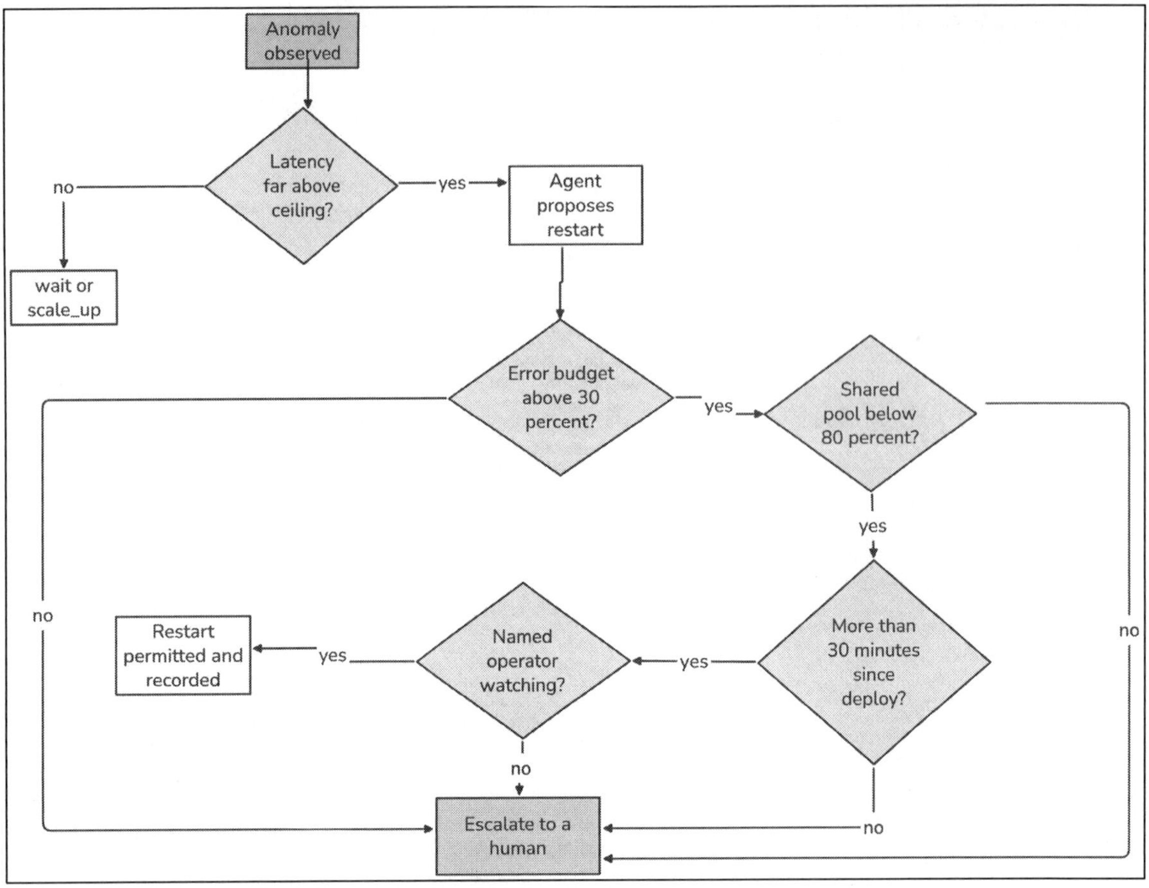

Measuring Agents Actions

Three Ways to Handle Same Anomaly

Our measurement reuses the serving engine we built earlier, which means a restart has genuine consequences rather than assumed ones. A **`restart`** method added to the engine drops every running and waiting request, marks each as truncated, and clears the cache. None of that is a simplification, since it is what a rolling restart does to work in flight.

The scenario raises arrival rate from 0.10 to 0.26 at tick 1500 and lets the system reach its new steady state. Our agent observes at tick 2400, reading a queue wait percentile over the preceding window exactly as a human reading a dashboard would. We then run three modes against identical traffic, namely no agent at all, an ungated agent, and a gated one.

```
python3 -m probes.remediation_run --agents 1
```

```
mode           action      delivered  truncated  rejected  goodput
```

```
ungated  escalated
------------------------------------------------------------------
---------------
unattended  none              594          0          407     0.575
0           0
ungated      restart          579         30          392    0.5605
1           0
             reason: latency far above ceiling
gated        escalate         594          0          407     0.575
0           1
             reason: error budget at 0.18
```

Our unattended run is the control, where a load anomaly produced 407 rejections and zero truncations. The admission control did its job, and every accepted request completed. The ungated agent then restarted the service, destroying thirty requests in flight and delivering fifteen fewer responses overall. The goodput fell from 0.575 to 0.5605.

No part of the restart addressed the actual problem, which was arrival rate rather than a stuck process. Our agent had no way to know that, since its policy maps a latency symptom to an action without any model of cause. The gated run behaved identically to the unattended one and additionally escalated to a human, because the error budget sat at 0.18 against a floor of 0.30.

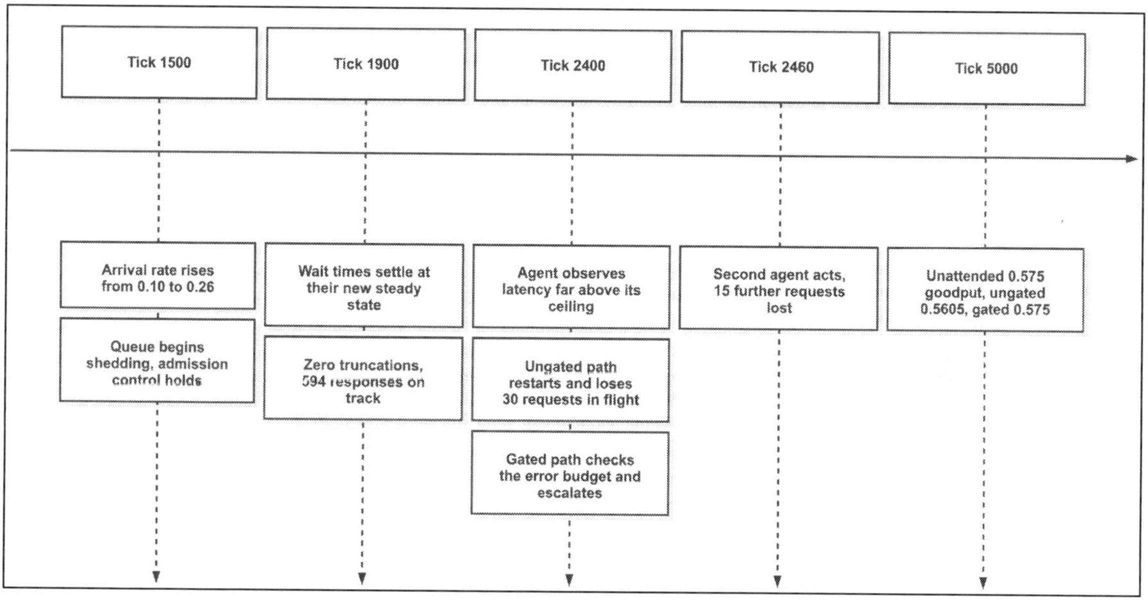

Multiple Agents and Single Shared Dependency

A single agent produces a single restart. Most organisations rarely stop at one, since a platform team, a serving team, and a data team all reasonably want their own automation. The same anomaly run with two and then three independent agents shows what happens when none of them knows about the others.

```
agents    delivered    truncated    goodput
     1          579           30     0.5605
     2          572           45     0.5537
     3          561           61     0.5431
```

The damage rises monotonically with every agent added, and goodput falls steadily away from the unattended baseline of 0.575. Each agent observed a real anomaly, chose a defensible action, and made the situation slightly worse than the agent before it. No individual decision was wrong by its own policy, and the combined blast radius belonged to nobody.

Action Ledger

A record of agent actions in the same place as injected faults costs a few lines and changes what a review can see. Our ledger writes one entry per action, carrying the tick, the actor, the chosen action, the reason, whether a gate intervened, and how many requests were lost.


```
[
  {
    "mode": "ungated",
    "tick": 2400,
    "actor": "remediation-agent-1",
    "action": "restart",
    "reason": "latency far above ceiling",
    "gated": false,
    "requests_lost": 30
  },
  {
    "mode": "ungated",
    "tick": 2460,
    "actor": "remediation-agent-2",
    "action": "restart",
    "reason": "latency far above ceiling",
    "gated": false,
    "requests_lost": 15
  }
]
```


Without that record, a postmortem sees a latency anomaly followed by two service restarts, and reasonably concludes that somebody restarted the service in response. The attribution to an agent, and the fact that the restarts cost forty five requests rather than saving anything, exists nowhere. Our ledger belongs in **`results`** alongside the experiment records, since the questions asked of both are identical.

Signals, Verdicts and Findings

Two New Agent Signals

Our envelope file gains two entries and rises to schema seven. A **`cascade_depth`** ceiling of 1.0 catches pipeline propagation, since a healthy pipeline averages 0.66 stages carrying wrong facts and a single injection pushes that to 2.99. An **`ungated_action_rate`** ceiling of zero catches autonomous actions taken without passing the gate, and zero is the only defensible value.

Both sit in the agent layer, which is not a reporting layer. The placement follows the rule we established for artifacts and have applied since, namely that a signal reports only when its breach produces a visible symptom on its own. Neither a compounding pipeline nor an ungated restart announces itself, so neither belongs among the signals that mark a result as reported.

Recording Findings

Fault	Tool	Signal watched	Verdict	Finding
One wrong fact injected at triage	Pipeline harness	cascade_depth, golden_set_score	Silent	Success fell 89.7 to 53.0 percent, amplified 2.01 times by the draft stage
Ungated agent restarts under load	Remediation harness	ungated_action_rate, truncated_valid_rate	Silent	Thirty requests destroyed, goodput fell 0.575 to 0.5605, restart addressed nothing
Three agents acting independently	Remediation harness	ungated_action_rate, truncated_valid_rate	Silent	Damage rose monotonically to 61 requests, no single decision was wrong
Same agent with the gate enabled	Remediation harness	ungated_action_rate, escalation_rate	Absorbed	Error budget at 0.18 blocked the action, outcome matched the unattended control exactly
Tool registry unreachable	Agent client	response_validity, retry_amplification	Cascaded	Detected every time, three retries per request, failure loud and immediate

Our three silent rows and one absorbed row tell the same story from opposite directions. Our gated run is the only configuration in this chapter that changed nothing about the outcome, which is precisely what a well governed agent should do when it has nothing useful to contribute. In the next chapter, we move to the training pipeline, where the actions are slower, more expensive, and considerably harder to reverse.

Summary

We measured propagation rather than assuming it. A single wrong fact entering a three stage pipeline became 2.16 wrong facts at the draft, reached all three stages in 2.99 runs out of three, and cut task success from 89.7 percent to 53.0. The amplification held near two across every injection level, so any review process sized against the original error will catch roughly half of what arrives.

Our remediation agent then demonstrated the reframing this book has been building toward. Faced with a load anomaly that admission control was already handling, it restarted the service, destroyed thirty requests in flight, and reduced goodput. Further agents added further damage, monotonically, with no individual decision being wrong. A gate checking error budget, dependency saturation, deploy recency, and operator presence produced an outcome identical to leaving the system alone. In Chapter 10 we turn to training.

Chapter 10
Distributed Training and Choas Fine-Tuning

In Chapter 9 we ended with a remediation agent that destroyed thirty requests in flight while trying to help, and a gate that produced an outcome identical to leaving the system alone. Every action there took seconds and cost a handful of responses. We now move to the layer where a single mistake costs a weekend of accelerator time and cannot be undone by restarting anything.

Across this chapter, we will build a small deterministic training run and prove that a resumed run is the same run, then measure exactly what breaks when a checkpoint omits any part of its state. The synchronous case follows, where one slow worker sets the pace and one dead worker sets it forever. We then compare two kinds of bad data, one loud and harmless and one quiet and permanent. Our closing section turns checkpoint cadence into arithmetic, since the right answer is neither as often as possible nor as rarely as you can bear.

Why Training Faults are Different?

Slow, Expensive and Hard to Reverse

Every layer so far has offered a fast feedback loop. An injected fault produced a measurable effect within minutes, and reverting it restored the previous behaviour completely. The training layer offers neither property. A fault injected at hour two of a fourteen hour run may not become visible until the evaluation at the end, and by then the damage sits inside the weights rather than in a queue somewhere.

The cost changes the design of experiments here more than anywhere else in the book. A chaos experiment against an inference service costs a few minutes of degraded traffic. The same experiment against a training job costs the accelerator hours consumed before the fault, plus everything consumed afterwards proving the outcome. Our earlier habit of sweeping a parameter across eight values becomes unaffordable at this layer, so every experiment has to justify itself before it starts. The reversibility disappears almost entirely. A corrupted batch absorbed into the weights cannot be extracted, and the only remedy is resuming from a checkpoint taken before the corruption arrived. Such a remedy depends on two things being true, namely that a suitable checkpoint exists and that resuming from it actually reproduces the run. We established for artifacts that internal consistency and correctness are different properties. The same distinction applies with more force to checkpoints.

Layer Failure without Failing

This layer shares the property that has driven the whole book, and takes it further than any layer we have measured. A distributed job under a straggler completes successfully, produces valid weights, and passes its evaluation. No error appears, no alert fires, and the only symptom is that it took four hours longer than it should have. A team comparing wall clock against a recorded baseline notices immediately, and nobody records that baseline. Far worse than a straggler is a worker that stops responding entirely. The synchronous loop waits at every collective operation for all participants, so one silent worker halts the job without raising an exception anywhere. Our remaining accelerators sit idle at full cost, the job looks alive to every scheduler and dashboard, and the failure resolves only when somebody notices the step counter has not moved.

A single consequence shapes the rest of this chapter. Our envelopes need signals that compare against recorded expectation rather than against absolute thresholds, because almost nothing at this layer has a natural bad value. A step time of 0.67 seconds is fine or terrible depending entirely on what it was yesterday.

Resumed Run Is Same Run

Everything That Influences Next

The checkpoint fidelity is testable, and the test is simpler than most teams expect. We run a job for six hundred steps and record the loss at every step. We checkpoint at step three hundred, restore, and run the remaining three hundred again. We then subtract the two trajectories. A correct checkpoint produces a difference of exactly zero, since floating point arithmetic is deterministic given identical inputs.

That zero requires saving everything that influences the next step, which is more than most checkpoint routines contain. The weights are obvious. The optimiser momentum is usually remembered. A further two pieces get forgotten regularly, namely the state of the generator that shuffles each epoch and the position within the current epoch. Both determine which samples arrive next, so omitting either produces a different sequence of batches from the moment of resumption.

That done, here's what we need in the training state at **app/training.py**:

```
@dataclass
class TrainState:
    w1: np.ndarray
    b1: np.ndarray
    w2: np.ndarray
    b2: np.ndarray
    m1: np.ndarray = field(default=None)
    mb1: np.ndarray = field(default=None)
    m2: np.ndarray = field(default=None)
    mb2: np.ndarray = field(default=None)
    step: int = 0
    epoch: int = 0
    cursor: int = 0
    order: np.ndarray = field(default=None)
    bit_generator_state: dict = field(default=None)


def new_epoch_order(state: TrainState, rows: int) -> None:
```

```
    rng = np.random.default_rng()
    rng.bit_generator.state = state.bit_generator_state
    state.order = rng.permutation(rows)
    state.bit_generator_state = rng.bit_generator.state
    state.cursor = 0
    state.epoch += 1
```

The generator restored from saved state rather than reseeded is the part that makes the whole thing work. A reseed produces a valid sequence and a different one, which is precisely the failure we are trying to detect. A determinism check before any experiment takes one line, and running the same three hundred steps twice produced a maximum difference of exactly zero.

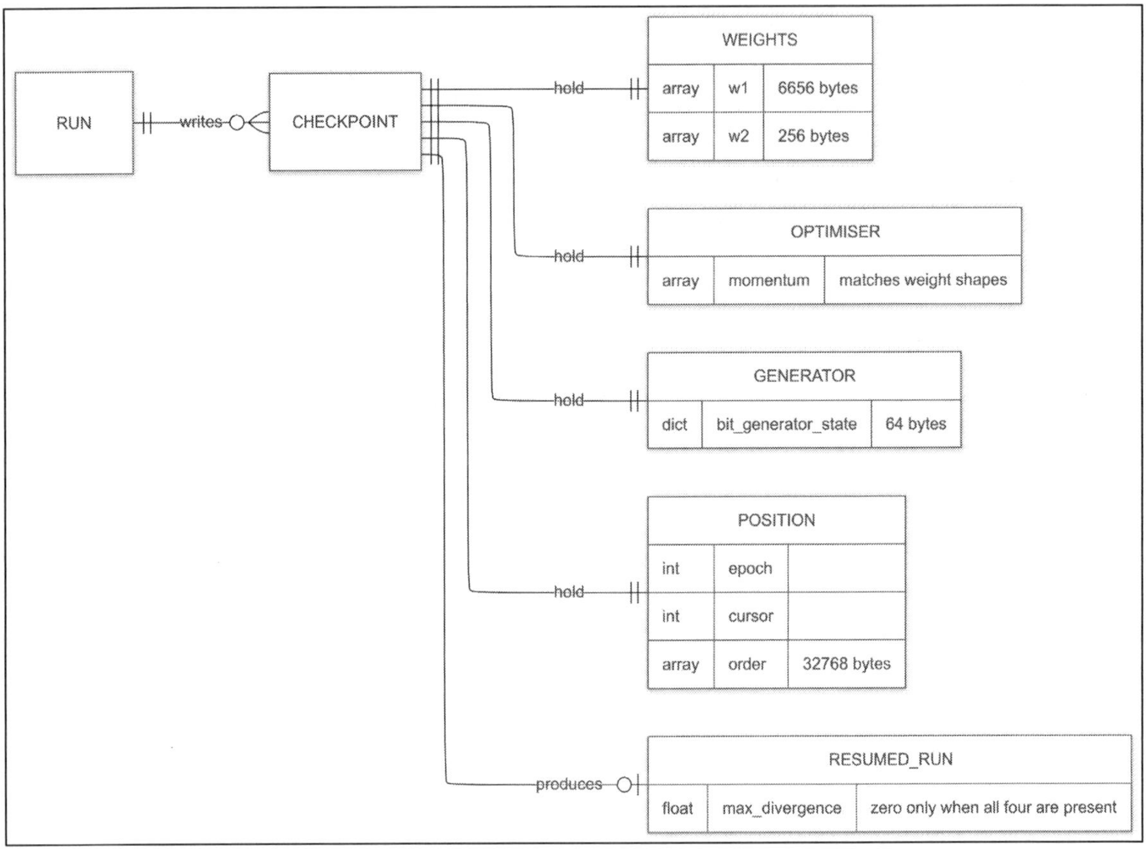

Five Checkpoints

We test five completeness levels against the same reference trajectory. Our full checkpoint holds all four categories. The four partial checkpoints each omit one piece, and the smallest holds weights alone, which is what a surprising number of production routines actually save.

```
python3 -m probes.checkpoint_fidelity
```

```
reference run, final loss 0.061253 after 600 steps
checkpoint holds  bytes kept   max divergence   final delta
outcome
------------------------------------------------------------------
---------
full                 46352        0.000e+00        0.000e+00
identical
no-generator         46288        2.553e-01        6.073e-02
DIVERGED
no-position          13456        2.256e-01        1.247e-02
DIVERGED
no-optimiser         39688        7.153e-02        1.295e-02
DIVERGED
weights-only          6728        2.316e-01        5.411e-02
DIVERGED
```

The gap between the first two rows is sixty four bytes. Our full checkpoint occupies 46,352 bytes and reproduces the reference trajectory exactly. The generator state dropped saves 64 bytes, which is fourteen hundredths of one percent of the file, and produces a maximum divergence of 0.2553. That fraction omitted destroys reproducibility as thoroughly as omitting eighty five percent of the file.

Every partial checkpoint diverges, and the sizes tell an uncomfortable story about what teams optimise. The weights alone occupy 6,728 bytes and look admirably lean. Everything needed for correctness costs seven times that in our toy model and a far smaller multiple in a real one, since real weights dwarf the shuffling order. Nobody saves an incomplete checkpoint to save space. They save one because nobody wrote down what the complete list contains.

A practical consequence follows directly. Any team relying on checkpoints for recovery should run this comparison once against their own training loop, because the outcome is binary and takes an afternoon. Either the divergence is zero or the checkpoint does not do what its name implies.

Synchronous Training

Stragglers

The synchronous data parallel loop waits for every worker at each collective operation, so step time is set by the slowest participant rather than by the average. Such an arrangement is efficient when workers are identical and punishing when they are not. A thermal variation, a noisy neighbour, or a slightly older accelerator all produce the same shape.

```
python3 -m probes.sync_training --workers 8 --steps 2000
```

8 workers, synchronous, 2000 steps

straggler	step time	wall clock	ratio	utilisation	wasted wh
1.00	0.4857	971.4	1.055	0.8315	0.364
1.15	0.5247	1049.3	1.142	0.7842	0.503
1.50	0.6661	1332.2	1.489	0.6442	1.053
2.00	0.8681	1736.3	1.985	0.5234	1.839
3.00	1.2722	2544.4	2.978	0.3969	3.410

A worker only fifteen percent slower than its peers costs eight percent of wall clock and five points of utilisation, which nobody would ever chase down. A worker half again as slow drops utilisation from 83 percent to 64 percent, so roughly a third of the fleet is idle at any moment while the job appears entirely healthy. At double speed the fleet is half wasted.

Our **straggler_ratio** signal tracks the slowest worker against the median, and it moves cleanly with the fault while wall clock alone does not. A team monitoring only step time sees a number that drifted upward and has no way to know whether the cause is a straggler, a larger batch, or a busier cluster. A recorded ratio separates the three immediately.

Worker that Stops without Crashing

A straggler wastes a fraction. A worker that stops responding entirely wastes everything, and does so without producing an error anybody can alert on. Our collective operation blocks waiting for a participant that will never arrive, every other accelerator sits idle at full cost, and the job remains in a running state as far as the scheduler is concerned.

one worker stops responding, no exception raised anywhere

watchdog	detected after	wasted worker hours	outcome
60s	60.0	0.13	watchdog fired
300s	300.0	0.67	watchdog fired
1800s	1800.0	4.00	watchdog fired
none	21600.0	48.00	job wall clock exhausted

The last row read against the first tells the story. With no watchdog, an eight worker job burns its entire six hour allocation and delivers nothing, wasting forty eight accelerator hours. A sixty second watchdog cuts that to 0.13 hours, which is a factor of three hundred and sixty nine from a single configuration line. No part of the watchdog is sophisticated, since it only needs to notice that the step counter has not advanced.

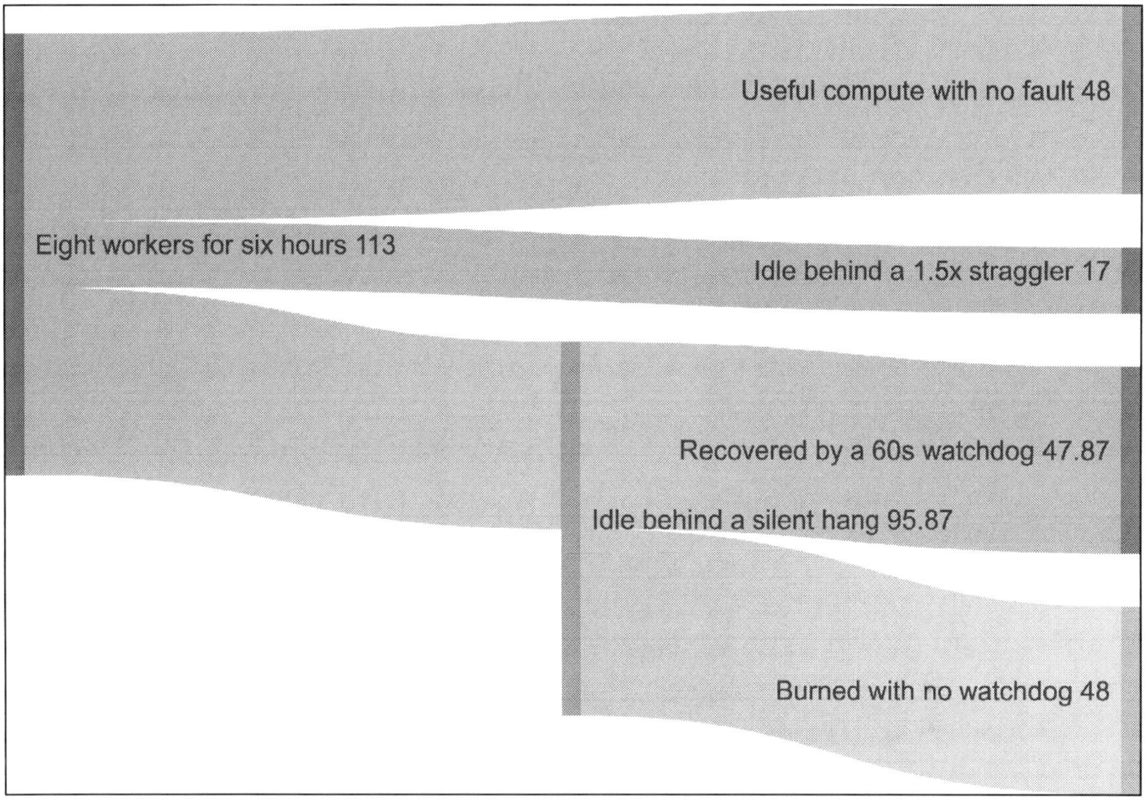

Every scheduler we have worked with treats a running job as a healthy job. A liveness check at the process level says nothing about progress, and progress is the only property that matters here. Our **`training_utilisation`** signal carries a floor of 0.80 for exactly this reason, since a hung job reports zero utilisation while reporting perfect health everywhere else.

Bad Data, Loud and Quiet

Transient Burst

The phrase bad data hides two failure modes, and they behave in opposite directions. A transient burst arrives when one shard is corrupt during one pass and never again, perhaps because a storage read returned zeros. Our harness flips every label for a window of steps in the middle of training.

transient burst, one shard arrives corrupt then never again

burst steps	peak train loss	train loss end	accuracy	delta
4	11.2120	0.0104	0.9629	-0.0029
30	11.2120	0.0180	0.9697	0.0039
60	11.2120	0.0124	0.9658	0.0000

The training loss spiked from under one to 11.2120, which is a rise of more than a thousand percent and visible on any loss chart from across a room. The holdout accuracy afterwards was entirely unaffected, moving by less than half a percentage point in either direction across every burst length tested. Such a fault is loud and harmless, since the optimiser simply recovers over the following steps.

Shard in Rotation every Epoch

A persistent corruption behaves in exactly the opposite way, and it is by far the more common failure. A shard whose labels are wrong is part of the dataset rather than an event, so it arrives again on every epoch. Our harness poisons a fixed fraction of rows permanently.

```
persistent poison, a fraction of rows carry wrong labels every
epoch
    fraction    peak train loss   train loss end  accuracy     delta
--------------------------------------------------------------------
        0.02             0.9935            0.1310    0.9697    0.0039
        0.05             0.9549            0.2979    0.9746    0.0088
        0.10             0.9007            0.2782    0.9629   -0.0029
        0.20             1.0114            0.5609    0.9395   -0.0264
```

The peak training loss never exceeded 1.0114 at any poison level, which is indistinguishable from the 0.9955 a clean run reaches on its first step. No spike appears anywhere, so nothing on a loss chart draws attention. The holdout accuracy holds up remarkably well too, staying within a percentage point of clean until the poison reaches twenty percent of the dataset.

A single column does move, and it is the one nobody looks at in isolation. The training loss at the end of the run rises from 0.0071 on a clean dataset to 0.1310 at two percent poison, and to 0.5609 at twenty percent. That is a seventy nine fold increase, and the absolute value of 0.5609 still looks like a perfectly ordinary training loss. Only comparison against a recorded baseline reveals it, which is the argument our steady state work made about every signal in this book.

Our **`train_loss_ratio`** signal exists for that reason, carrying a ceiling of three against a recorded baseline rather than an absolute threshold. A team without such a baseline has no mechanism to detect a poisoned shard short of auditing the data by hand.

Cost-aware Experiment Design

Checkpoint Cadence against Preemption

The checkpoint cadence is usually chosen by instinct, and instinct picks a round number. We turn it into arithmetic with four inputs, namely step duration, checkpoint duration, restart duration, and how often preemption occurs. The expected lost work per preemption is half the cadence, since preemption arrives uniformly between checkpoints.

```
python3 -m probes.spot_cadence --steps 200000 --preempt-per-hour
0.35
```

```
200000 steps at 0.46s, 0.35 preemptions per hour
  cadence  checkpoints  overhead h   lost h  restart h   total h
efficiency
------------------------------------------------------------------
---------
      250          800         9.33     0.14       0.45     35.48
0.7203
      500          400         4.67     0.29       0.45     30.96
0.8256
     1000          200         2.33     0.57       0.45     28.91
0.8840
     2500           80         0.93     1.43       0.45     28.36
0.9010
     5000           40         0.47     2.86       0.45     29.33
0.8714
    20000           10         0.12    11.43       0.45     37.55
0.6806
```

The efficiency traces a clean curve with an optimum at 2,500 steps, where the job completes in 28.36 hours at ninety percent efficiency. A checkpoint every 250 steps feels prudent and costs 9.33 hours of pure overhead, dropping efficiency to 72 percent. A checkpoint every 20,000 steps feels lean and loses 11.43 hours to redone work, landing at 68 percent.

Both extremes cost roughly the same, which is the useful observation. Our worst cadence is nine hours worse than our best, on a job that should take twenty five and a half hours of pure compute. Nobody would accept a thirty five percent overhead knowingly, and plenty of teams carry one because the number was chosen once and never revisited.

A caveat belongs alongside those figures. Every input is measurable on any real job in under an hour, so there is no reason to run this with guessed numbers. The preemption rate in particular varies enormously by region and instance type, and using a published average rather than your own observation will move the optimum by a factor of several.

Recording Findings

Fault	Tool	Signal watched	Verdict	Finding
Checkpoint omits generator state	Training harness	resume_divergence	Silent	Sixty four bytes missing produced 0.2553 divergence, resumption is not resumption

One worker running at 1.5x	Sync harness	straggler_ratio, training_utilisation	Silent	Utilisation fell 0.83 to 0.64, job completed successfully four hours late
One worker stops responding, no watchdog	Sync harness	training_utilisation	Silent	Forty eight accelerator hours burned, job reported running throughout
Same hang with a sixty second watchdog	Sync harness	training_utilisation	Absorbed	Detected in sixty seconds, 0.13 hours wasted, a factor of 369 improvement
Transient corrupt burst, sixty steps	Training harness	train_loss_ratio	Absorbed	Loss spiked to 11.21 and recovered fully, holdout accuracy unchanged
Poisoned shard at twenty percent	Training harness	train_loss_ratio	Silent	No loss spike anywhere, final training loss seventy nine times the baseline
Checkpoint write fails mid epoch	Training harness	checkpoint_write_success	Degraded	The only training fault in this chapter that announces itself

All but one of the seven rows are either silent or absorbed, and the single degraded row is the one where an operating system returned an error. Every other fault at this layer completed successfully by every conventional measure. In Chapter 11 we turn to the question this table raises, namely how anybody is supposed to see any of it.

Summary

We proved that a resumed run can be identical to the run it continues, and measured precisely what it costs to get that wrong. The four categories of state all matter, and omitting the smallest of them, sixty four bytes of generator state out of forty six thousand, produced a divergence indistinguishable from throwing the checkpoint away. Any team relying on checkpoints for recovery can settle the question in an afternoon, and the outcome is binary.

The synchronous loop then showed how a fifteen percent straggler costs five points of utilisation and a silent hang costs everything, with a sixty second watchdog separating 48 wasted accelerator hours from 0.13. The phrase bad data proved to cover two opposite personalities, where a transient burst spiked the loss a thousandfold and did no lasting harm, while a persistent poisoned shard produced no spike at all and left final training loss seventy nine times its baseline. In Chapter

11 we take up observability.

CHAPTER 11
OBSERVING PROBABILISTIC DEGRADATION

In Chapter 10 we closed with six training faults out of seven landing on silent or absorbed, and a single degraded row where an operating system happened to return an error. Our nine chapters of experiments have now produced a great many results that nothing in the system announced. This chapter takes up the obvious question, namely how anybody is supposed to see any of it.

Across this chapter, we will put the detector every earlier chapter relied on under proper measurement and find it wanting. A second detector follows, one that accumulates departure rather than watching a line, and the difference in time to detection runs to a factor of eight. Our attention then turns to the observing path itself, where five injected faults produce five silent verdicts and an eighth layer joins the taxonomy. The attribution problem closes the chapter, since a naive before and after comparison can double the effect it reports.

Detector In Use So Far

What Threshold Can See?

Every experiment so far has used the same detection rule. A signal breaches when a sampled value falls outside its envelope, and we require two consecutive samples to avoid firing on noise. Such a rule is simple, explicable, and correct for the faults it was designed against. Our serving experiments broke stream completion from 1.0 to 0.8525 in a single step, which no threshold could miss.

The rule is limited by two properties, and both matter more at this layer than anywhere else. A threshold has no memory, so ten consecutive samples one thousandth below the mean carry exactly the same weight as one sample. A threshold also has no notion of expectation, since it compares against a fixed bound rather than against what the signal was doing yesterday. Both limitations point at the same blind spot. Our envelopes were derived with deliberate slack on top of the bootstrap interval, precisely so that ordinary variation would not fire them. That slack is the gap a slow degradation lives in. A signal drifting steadily downward inside its envelope produces no alert at all until it finally crosses the floor, by which time the drift has been running for however long the slack allowed.

Accumulating Departure

A cumulative sum detector solves the memory problem directly. Rather than asking whether this sample is outside the bound, it asks how much total departure from baseline has accumulated. Small allowances of slack absorb ordinary noise, and anything persistent adds up regardless of how small each contribution is.

The detector takes two parameters. The slack sets how much departure per sample gets forgiven, expressed in standard deviations so the setting transfers between signals. The limit sets how much accumulated departure triggers the alarm. A slack of half a standard deviation with the limit at five works well across every signal we have measured, and neither figure is delicate.

Both detectors then go into **probes/detect.py** like this:

```
"""Two detectors. One watches a line, the other watches an
accumulation."""
from __future__ import annotations

from dataclasses import dataclass, field


@dataclass
class ThresholdDetector:
    """Fires when a sample crosses the envelope. What every chapter
has used so far."""
    floor: float | None = None
    ceiling: float | None = None
    consecutive: int = 2
    _run: int = 0

    def observe(self, value: float) -> bool:
        breached = (
            (self.floor is not None and value < self.floor)
            or (self.ceiling is not None and value > self.ceiling)
        )
        self._run = self._run + 1 if breached else 0
        return self._run >= self.consecutive


@dataclass
class CusumDetector:
    """Fires when accumulated departure from baseline exceeds a
budget.

    Slack absorbs ordinary noise. Anything persistent adds up
regardless of size.
    """
    baseline: float
    sigma: float
    direction: str = "down"          # which way counts as worse
    slack_sigmas: float = 0.5
    limit_sigmas: float = 5.0
    total: float = 0.0
    history: list[float] = field(default_factory=list)

    def observe(self, value: float) -> bool:
        slack = self.slack_sigmas * self.sigma
        departure = (
```

```
            self.baseline - value if self.direction == "down" else
value - self.baseline
        )
        self.total = max(0.0, self.total + departure - slack)
        self.history.append(self.total)
        return self.total > self.limit_sigmas * self.sigma
```

The cumulative detector needs a baseline and a standard deviation, which the threshold detector does not. Both come free from our original derivation work, since the bootstrap already produced them. A reader who skipped that chapter has no baseline to compare against and therefore cannot run this detector at all, which is one more argument for doing the measurement work first.

Measuring Detection Latency

Step Changes

Our test drives a synthetic recall signal at the derived baseline of 0.8035 with a standard deviation of 0.012, sampled every five minutes. A fault arrives at a fixed point and drops the mean by a chosen amount. Some two hundred trials per configuration give a stable median for how long each detector takes to notice.

```
python3 -m probes.detection_latency
```

```
recall baseline 0.8035, floor 0.733, sample every 5 minutes
shape          drop     threshold  hit rate         cusum  hit rate
-------------------------------------------------------------------
step          0.020         never      0.00        15 min      1.00
step          0.050      1010 min      0.64         5 min      1.00
step          0.090         5 min      1.00         0 min      1.00
step          0.150         5 min      1.00         0 min      1.00
```

The bottom two rows carry the good news. A drop of 0.09 or more crosses the floor immediately, and both detectors fire within one sample. No part of this chapter argues against thresholds for faults of that size, since a threshold is cheaper to reason about and equally fast.

The top two rows are the problem. A drop of 0.02 never fires the threshold at all across two hundred trials, because 0.7835 sits comfortably inside a floor of 0.733. Our cumulative detector notices in fifteen minutes with perfect reliability. A drop of 0.05 fires the threshold in sixteen hours and only in two thirds of trials, against five minutes and every trial for the alternative.

Slow Ramps

A step change flatters the threshold, since a fault that arrives all at once either crosses the bound or does not. Actual degradation at this layer arrives as a ramp. An index ages one document at a time, a shard poisons a growing fraction of batches, and a thermal problem worsens across an afternoon.

ramp	0.020	never	0.00	565 min	1.00
ramp	0.050	2560 min	0.03	345 min	1.00
ramp	0.090	1775 min	1.00	230 min	1.00
ramp	0.150	1122 min	1.00	165 min	1.00

Every row here is worse than its step equivalent, and the gap between detectors widens rather than narrowing. A ramp reaching 0.09 takes the threshold 1,775 minutes, which is a little under thirty hours. Our cumulative detector reaches the same conclusion in 230 minutes, so the ratio is 7.7 to one. At a ramp of 0.15, an unmistakable collapse, the threshold still needs nearly nineteen hours.

The 0.05 ramp deserves particular attention. Our retrieval work established that quality in that region pushes a system toward being worse than no retrieval at all. Our threshold detector finds it in three percent of trials, which is to say it does not find it. A team relying on envelope breaches alone would run a retrieval augmented service in that state indefinitely.

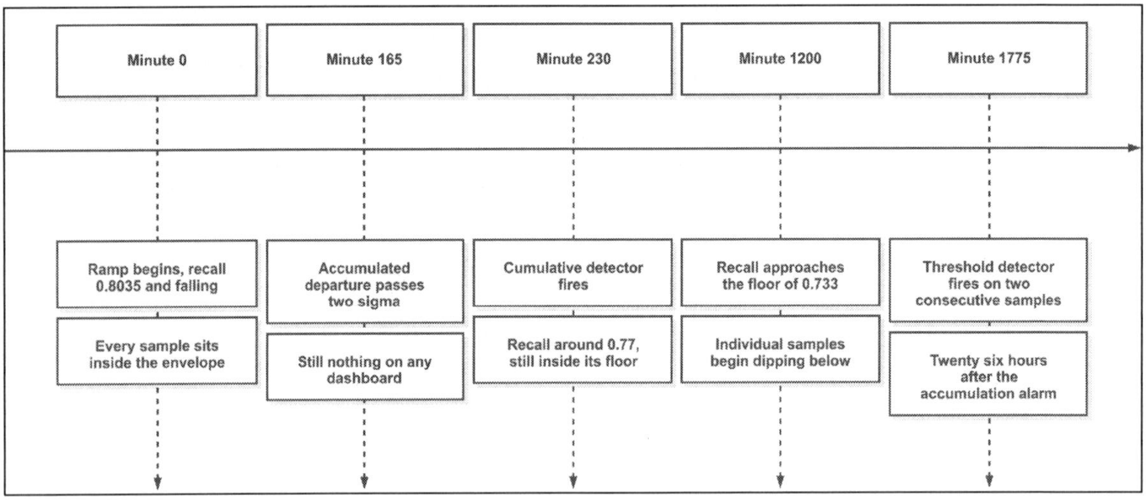

Our findings tables from Chapters 4 through 10 recorded whether a signal breached, which was the right question for the experiments we ran. Every one of those experiments injected a fault at full strength and held it, so the values moved in a single step and the threshold was adequate. No experiment in those chapters tested a fault that arrived gradually. The faults in production are not so obliging. The stale index, the poisoned shard from Chapter 10, and the thermal throttle all arrive as ramps in the real world and as steps in our lab. Our verdicts remain correct, and the detection latencies implied by them are optimistic by roughly an order of magnitude.

Breaking Observing Path

The Eighth Layer

Our original taxonomy named seven layers, all of which produce and serve model output. The observing path produces nothing a user consumes and therefore never appeared. The experiments since have made the omission untenable, since a measurement system that fails takes every one of those seven layers down with it silently.

An eighth layer forces one question immediately, namely whether observability belongs among the reporting layers. Our reporting set contains accelerator, serving, and artifact, on the grounds that each surfaces failure through ordinary errors. It cannot possibly qualify, because a monitoring system that has failed is by definition unable to report that it has failed. The self reference is exact rather than clever.

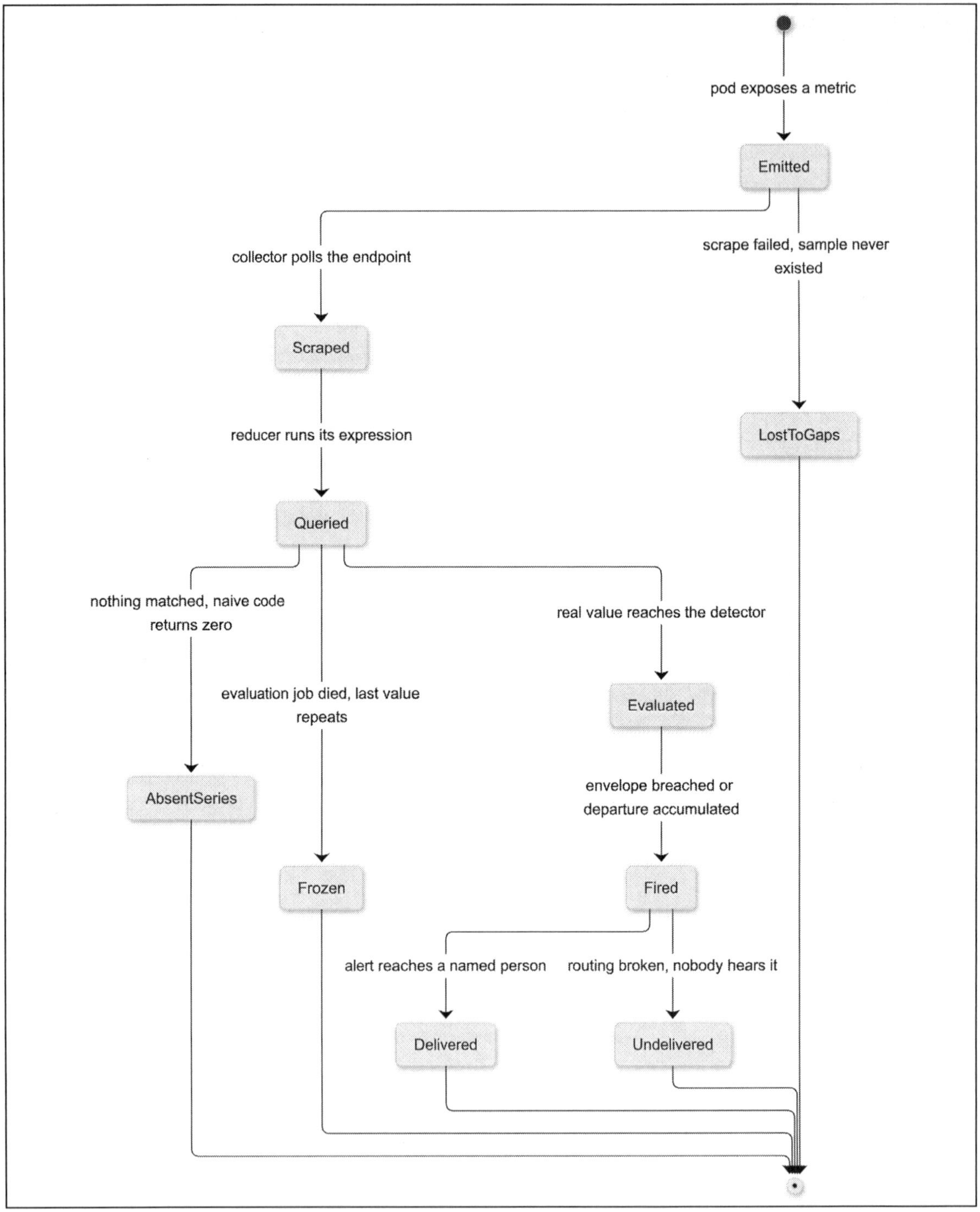

The path has four break points, and each defeats a different part of our machinery. A scrape gap removes samples before anything sees them. An absent series produces a value that is wrong rather than missing. A frozen evaluation job repeats the last good value forever. Broken alert routing lets the detector fire into silence.

Five Faults and Five Silent Verdicts

Our harness drives a real degradation while injecting each observability fault, then asks whether the detectors still notice. We test two signals, one carrying a floor and one carrying a ceiling, because the absent series fault behaves completely differently against each.

```
python3 -m probes.obs_chaos
```

```
recall_at_5, floor 0.733, a real shift of 0.09 is under way in
every row
observability fault   detected   median latency   freshness alarm
------------------------------------------------------------------
none                      1.00             0 min             never
scrape-gaps               1.00             0 min             never
absent-series             1.00             0 min             never
frozen-signal             0.00             never           120 min
alert-undelivered         0.00             never             never

override_rate, ceiling 0.085, a real shift of 0.08 is under way in
every row
observability fault   detected   median latency   freshness alarm
------------------------------------------------------------------
none                      1.00             0 min             never
scrape-gaps               1.00             0 min             never
absent-series             0.00             never             never
frozen-signal             0.00             never           120 min
alert-undelivered         0.00             never             never
```

The asymmetry in the absent series row across the two tables is the whole point. Under a floor, a missing series reducing to zero looks catastrophically low and fires immediately. Under a ceiling, the same zero looks perfectly healthy and never fires at all. We met this trap by accident while building the lab, when a relabelling mistake left Prometheus returning no series and every floor check passed. A full half of our signals carry ceilings, so half of them are exposed.

The scrape gaps at forty percent turned out to be harmless in both cases, which was not what we expected. A loss of two samples in five delays nothing measurably when the underlying shift is large, since the detectors simply work from the samples that survive. A team tempted to invest heavily in scrape reliability should test the assumption first, because the money is better spent elsewhere.

Freshness that Works

Our frozen signal fault defeats both detectors completely. An evaluation job that dies leaves its last published value in place, so every subsequent sample reads healthy forever. No threshold fires, no departure accumulates, and the graph is a perfectly flat line at exactly the right value. A single check catches it, and only one. The time since a signal last changed, or last received a genuinely new sample, exposes the freeze in two hours with our settings. Our new **signal_freshness_seconds** carries a ceiling of nine hundred, which is fifteen minutes, chosen so that a golden set job running every five minutes has room to be late twice.

The alert delivery defeats even that. Our final row shows a detector firing correctly into a routing configuration that goes nowhere, which is the failure we recorded in the lab when a job success alert pointed at an archived channel. No property distinguishes an alert that fired and was delivered from one that fired and vanished, unless delivery itself gets measured. Our **alert_delivery_rate** carries a floor of exactly one, since any other value means somebody is not being told something.

Attribution

Drift under Experiment

Every comparison in this book has taken the same shape, namely a baseline sample, an injection sample, and the difference between them. Such a comparison assumes the system would have stayed still had we not intervened. We spent an entire chapter on retrieval establishing that quality decays continuously whether anybody touches it or not.

An experiment run on top of an existing drift produces a delta that mixes two causes. Our harness measures how badly, by generating a baseline window that is already declining, injecting a known effect of exactly 0.040, and comparing the naive estimate against the truth.

```
python3 -m probes.attribution --injected 0.040
```

```
true injected effect 0.04, windows of 48 samples
  drift per day   naive estimate     error   trend corrected
error
------------------------------------------------------------------
---
          0.000            0.0399   -0.0001            0.0398    -
0.0002
         -0.010            0.0416    0.0016            0.0398    -
0.0002
         -0.030            0.0449    0.0049            0.0398    -
0.0002
         -0.060            0.0499    0.0099            0.0398    -
0.0002
```

-0.120	0.0599	0.0199	0.0398	-0.0002
-0.240	0.0799	0.0399	0.0398	-0.0002

With no drift, the naive estimate is accurate to a ten thousandth, which is reassuring and unsurprising. At a drift of 0.06 per day the naive estimate overstates the injected effect by twenty five percent. At 0.24 per day it reports exactly double, attributing a full 0.040 of pre-existing decay to an experiment that had nothing to do with it.

Correction for Trend

The bias needs no sophistication to fix. A line fitted through the baseline window and extrapolated across the injection window produces a prediction of what would have happened anyway. The observed values subtracted from that prediction isolate the injected effect. Our corrected column returns 0.0398 at every drift rate tested, including the most extreme. The accuracy holds because the correction removes exactly the component the drift contributed, leaving the injection alone. None of the technique requires more than a least squares fit over the samples already collected.

A pair of practical consequences follow for how we record results. Every experiment record should carry the baseline slope alongside the baseline mean, since a slope near zero means the naive delta is trustworthy and a steep one means it is not. Any experiment run against a signal with a meaningful slope should also report the corrected estimate rather than the raw difference, because a result that doubles a real effect will send somebody chasing the wrong cause for a week.

Findings

We have five faults and five silent verdicts, which is the only fully silent table in the book. None of that outcome is a modelling artefact, since a fault in the observing path cannot by construction report itself through the path it has broken. Every one of these failures is caught only by a check that sits outside the thing being checked.

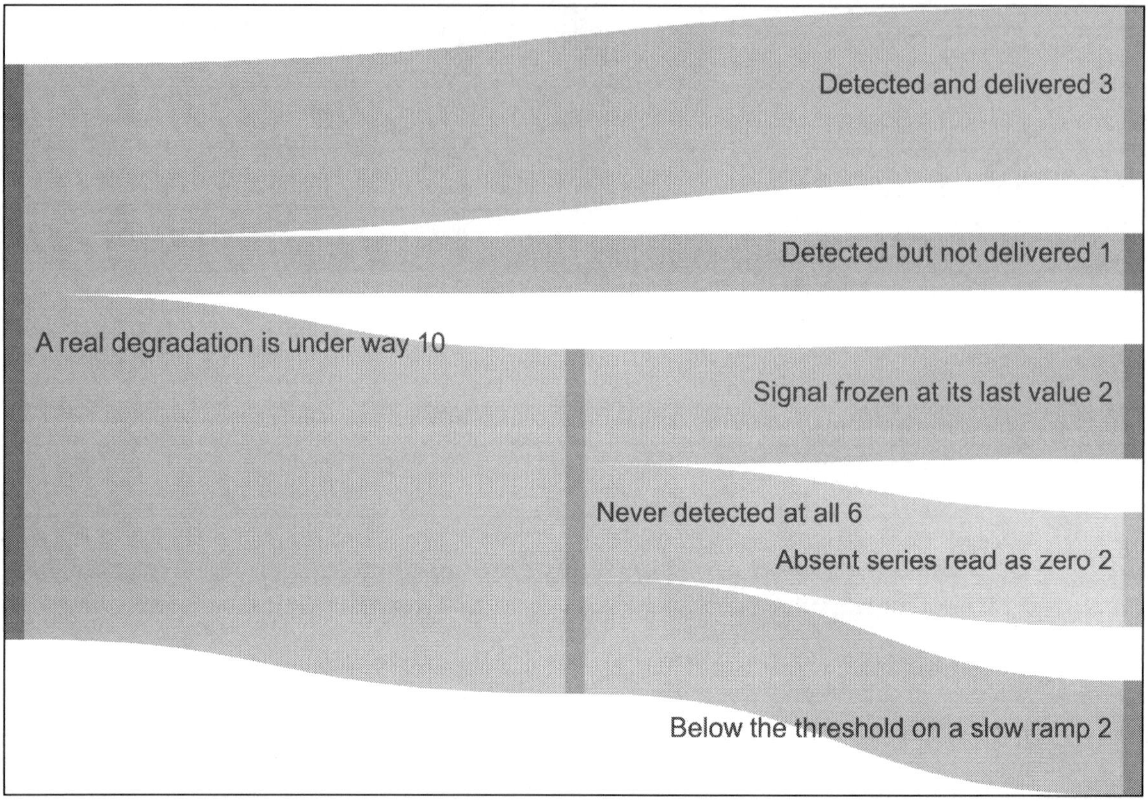

In Chapter 12 we gather every silent row from every chapter into one place and turn the collection into a programme. Our detection latency figures matter there too, since a silent result that a cumulative detector would have caught in four hours is a very different proposition from one nothing can catch at all.

Fault	Tool	Signal watched	Verdict	Finding
Scrape gaps at forty percent	Detection harness	scrape_completeness	Silent	Completeness fell to 0.60 and detection was unaffected, both detectors still fired at once
Absent series against a ceiling signal	Detection harness	detection_latency_minutes	Silent	Zero reads as healthy under a ceiling, a real rise of 0.08 was never detected
Evaluation job frozen	Detection harness	signal_freshness_seconds	Silent	Both detectors defeated completely, only the freshness check caught it, after 120 minutes
Alert routing	Detection	alert_delivery_rate	Silent	Detector fired correctly

broken	harness			every time, nobody was told, no check exists that notices
Threshold detector alone on a slow ramp	Detection harness	detection_latency_minutes	Silent	1,775 minutes against 230 for accumulated departure, a factor of 7.7

We avoided anomaly detection using learned models deliberately rather than for practical reasons. A cumulative sum detector needs two parameters and produces a result anybody can explain to an incident review. Every learned alternative we considered needs training data, periodic retraining, and an explanation nobody can give at three in the morning. A team with mature practice should certainly evaluate them, and a team without a baseline should build one first.

Summary

We measured the detector this book has relied on for nine chapters and found it adequate for exactly the faults we had been injecting. Under a step change of 0.09 or larger it fires within one sample. Under a slow ramp of the same size it takes nearly thirty hours, and against a drop of 0.02 it never fires at all. A cumulative sum detector, needing only the baseline and standard deviation our derivation already produced, reached the same conclusions between five and eight times faster.

Our faults in the observing path then produced the only fully silent findings table in the book. The scrape gaps at forty percent proved harmless, while a frozen evaluation job and an absent series against a ceiling signal both hid a real degradation completely. Broken alert routing defeated everything including the freshness check. The attribution problem closed the chapter, where a pre-existing drift of 0.24 per day caused a naive comparison to report exactly double the true injected effect, and a least squares correction removed the bias entirely. In Chapter 12 we turn all of it into a programme.

CHAPTER 12
OPERATIONALIZING CHAOS

In Chapter 11 we produced the only fully silent findings table in the book, where five faults in the observing path each hid a real degradation and none could report itself. Our eleven chapters of experiments now sit recorded on disk, each one a small JSON file carrying a verdict. This closing chapter reads all of them at once and turns the collection into something a team can run.

Across this chapter, we will roll up every experiment and find that nearly half landed on silent, well above the third Chapter 1 predicted. Our signal file gets audited against those results, showing how few of the silent findings the original eight signals could have caught. We then put three gates into a pipeline as one command, continuous chaos replaces the quarterly game day, and a ninety day roadmap closes the practical work. Our final section states plainly where this field stands today.

What Forty One Experiments Showed?

Roll-up

Every scoring tool in this book writes a record to **`results`**, carrying the injection layer, the signals that breached, whether the system reported the breach, and one verdict word. None of those records was designed for this chapter, which is exactly why the roll-up is worth trusting. They read back with no interpretation and no transcription.

We are ready to write the roll-up at **`probes/rollup.py`** and run its scorecard as below:

```
python3 -m probes.rollup --section scorecard
```

```
verdict          experiments     share
-----------------------------------
absorbed                   6     14.6%
degraded                   4      9.8%
cascaded                  11     26.8%
silent                    20     48.8%
-----------------------------------
total                     41    100.0%
```

In Chapter 1 we fixed the four word vocabulary and predicted that roughly one third of results would land on silent, adding that anything much lower would suggest the experiments were too gentle. The actual figure is 48.8 percent, so nearly half of everything we broke produced no signal the system itself would raise. Our prediction was not too aggressive. It was too conservative.

The rarest verdict is degraded at 9.8 percent, and its scarcity carries a message of its own. Only four experiments out of forty one produced a fault that the system noticed, contained within the layer where we injected it, and reported. Every other fault either vanished into tolerance, spread beyond its origin, or went unremarked. The outcome every reliability programme aims for is containment with notification, and it is the least common thing we observed.

```
python3 -m probes.rollup --section coverage
```

```
injected at      experiments  silent  symptoms appeared at
--------------------------------------------------------------------
-----------
accelerator                3       1  accelerator x2, serving x1,
boundary x1, retrieval x1
agent                      5       3  agent x4, boundary x4
artifact                   4       1  artifact x2, serving x1,
boundary x1
boundary                   8       3  agent x7, boundary x6
observability              5       5  observability x5
retrieval                  5       2  boundary x4, retrieval x3
serving                    4       1  serving x2, boundary x2
training                   7       4  training x5
```

In Chapter 1 we argued that a fault injected at one layer routinely surfaces at another, and that a map connecting the two saves a day of debugging prompts while the cause sits in a power limit. That column now has evidence behind it. The accelerator faults produced symptoms at four different layers. The boundary faults produced symptoms at the agent layer seven times against six at their own. Only observability faults stayed put, for reasons that layer cannot help.

Signals that Worked

Our signal file began Chapter 2 with eight measurements and ends at thirty five across eight layers. The twenty seven additions over ten chapters felt reasonable at each step and look extravagant in aggregate, so the roll-up should be asked whether they earned their place.

```
python3 -m probes.rollup --section signals
```

```
signal                           silent results it caught
-------------------------------------------------------
truncated_valid_rate                                   4  (added
after Chapter 2)
detection_latency_minutes                              4  (added
after Chapter 2)
golden_set_score                                       3  (added
after Chapter 2)
recall_at_5                                            2
index_age_hours                                        2  (added
after Chapter 2)
unsupported_rate                                       2  (added
after Chapter 2)
tool_call_success                                      2
```

```
ungated_action_rate                                  2   (added
after Chapter 2)
training_utilisation                                 2   (added
after Chapter 2)
-------------------------------------------------------
caught by the original eight signals alone : 4 of 20
caught only by signals added later         : 16 of 20
```

Only four of twenty silent results would have been caught by the eight signals we derived in Chapter 2. The other sixteen required a signal that did not exist when the programme started. A reader stopping after the steady state chapter would have built something genuinely useful and would have missed four fifths of what the practice eventually found.

An implication deserves stating plainly, because it contradicts how signal files usually get built. A signal should be added in response to an experiment rather than in advance of one, since every one of those sixteen additions came from an experiment revealing that nothing existing could see the fault. Any attempt to enumerate the right thirty five signals up front is not merely hard. It is the wrong activity, because the list is a record of what you have learned rather than a specification of what you should measure.

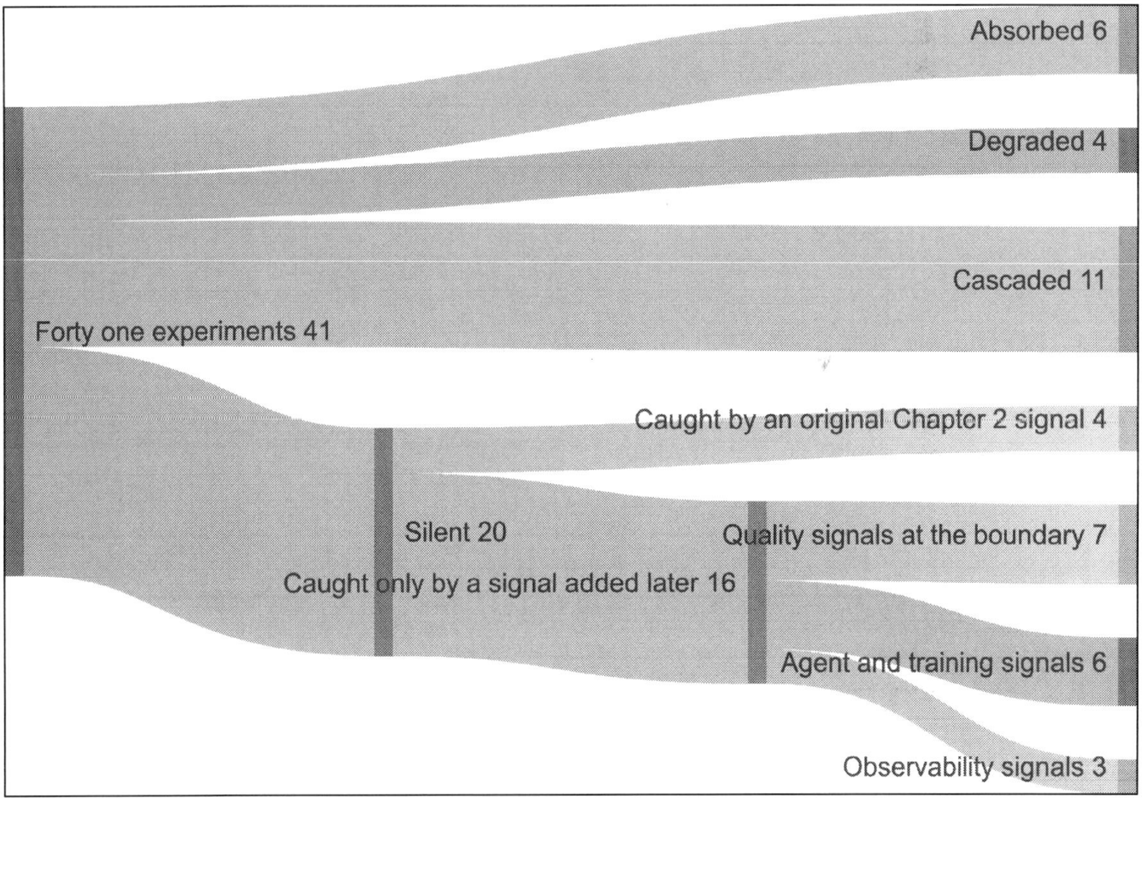

Putting Machinery in Pipeline

Three Gates and One Command

Every tool we built has run by hand so far, which is adequate for a book and inadequate for a team. The changes that can quietly invalidate the practice fall under three gates. Our chaos change gate verifies that the verdict rules still cover all four branches, that probe thresholds still match the committed envelopes, and that experiment specifications remain safe to schedule.

Our model change gate is the one most organisations lack entirely. The artifacts get verified against their recorded manifest, and the golden set gets scored per category rather than in aggregate. In Chapter 6 we established that an aggregate gate approves a release whose highest risk category has collapsed, so the per category comparison is the whole point.

Our steady state gate closes the loop by confirming that a healthy capture still sits inside every envelope. A failure there means either the system changed or the envelopes drifted, and both need somebody to look before any experiment runs.

So, here's what you need to write in the gate at **probes/pipeline_gate.sh**:

```
#!/usr/bin/env bash
# Every check that must pass before a chaos change or a model
change merges.
set -uo pipefail
FAILED=0

check() {
  local label="$1"; shift
  if "$@" > /tmp/gate.out 2>&1; then
    printf '  pass  %s\n' "$label"
  else
    printf '  FAIL  %s\n' "$label"
    sed 's/^/          /' /tmp/gate.out | tail -4
    FAILED=$((FAILED + 1))
  fi
}

echo "chaos change gate"
check "verdict rules cover all four branches" python3 -m
probes.test_verdict
for engine in experiments/exp-002-gateway-pod-delete.yaml
experiments/exp-004-node-drain.yaml; do
  check "probe thresholds match signals, ${engine##*/}" python3 -m
probes.sync_check "$engine"
done
```

```
check "experiment specification is safe to schedule" \
  python3 -m probes.validate_experiment experiments/exp-001-index-
staleness.yaml

echo "model change gate"
check "artifact matches its recorded manifest" \
  python3 -m probes.artifact_check artifacts/model-v1.safetensors \
  --manifest artifacts/model-v1.manifest.json
check "no golden set category regressed" python3 -m
probes.version_delta

echo "steady state gate"
check "healthy capture sits inside every envelope" \
  python3 -m probes.check --capture results/healthy-capture.jsonl

if [ "$FAILED" -gt 0 ]; then
  echo "gate rejected the change, ${FAILED} check(s) failed"
  exit 1
fi
echo "gate passed all checks"
```

A run against the repository as this book leaves it produces the outcome the whole exercise was for.

```
chaos change gate
  pass  verdict rules cover all four branches
  pass  probe thresholds match signals, exp-002-gateway-pod-
delete.yaml
  pass  probe thresholds match signals, exp-004-node-drain.yaml
  pass  experiment specification is safe to schedule
model change gate
  pass  artifact matches its recorded manifest
  FAIL  no golden set category regressed
        golden_set_score    : 0.93
        model_version_drift : 1
        regressed categories: settlements
steady state gate
  pass  healthy capture sits inside every envelope
gate rejected the change, 1 check(s) failed
```

That failing check is the Chapter 6 release whose aggregate score rose by one and a half points while settlement responses fell from 0.925 to 0.600. It shipped unnoticed six chapters ago. It now blocks a merge in under a second, on a laptop, with no cluster involved.

Staging and Exception

In Chapter 3 we chose a staging first posture and the roll-up supports it, with one important exception. The infrastructure faults reproduce faithfully in a shrunken environment, since topology rather than capacity determines how they propagate. Our accelerator, serving, artifact, and training experiments all behaved the same way at lab scale as they would at production scale, so running them against real traffic buys nothing but risk. The quality faults are different, and pretending otherwise would be dishonest. The retrieval staleness depends on how fast real documents change. The model version skew depends on what real users ask. The agent cascades depend on the actual distribution of tickets arriving. Every one of those experiments measures something about production data that a synthetic corpus cannot supply.

Our compromise runs those experiments against production traffic with a small fraction and a hard gate. We allow ten percent of requests, a named operator watching, error budget above thirty percent, and the abort thresholds from Chapter 2 set well outside the envelopes. A team unwilling to accept that exposure should accept instead that their retrieval and boundary layers are untested, since those are the only two positions available.

Running Chaos Continuously

Scheduled Experiments and Shared Budget

A quarterly game day produces a burst of learning and eleven weeks of decay. Our findings argue for the opposite cadence, because the failure modes that dominated this book accumulate slowly and hide in ordinary operation. A stale index, a poisoned shard, and a drifting model version all take weeks to matter, so an experiment schedule measured in weeks catches them and one measured in quarters does not.

The continuous version needs an accounting discipline that quarterly chaos does not. Multiple teams running experiments against overlapping dependencies produce a combined effect that no individual team planned, which Chapter 9 measured directly when three independent agents each made things slightly worse. Our answer is a single shared ledger recording every scheduled experiment alongside every autonomous action, checked before anything new starts. A further scheduling rule earned itself during this book. Any experiment that produced a silent verdict should re-run more often than those that produced anything else, because a silent result means the detection gap is still open. Anything that produced a degraded verdict has a working alert and can be tested annually. Our twenty silent rows therefore set the schedule, and the four degraded rows do not.

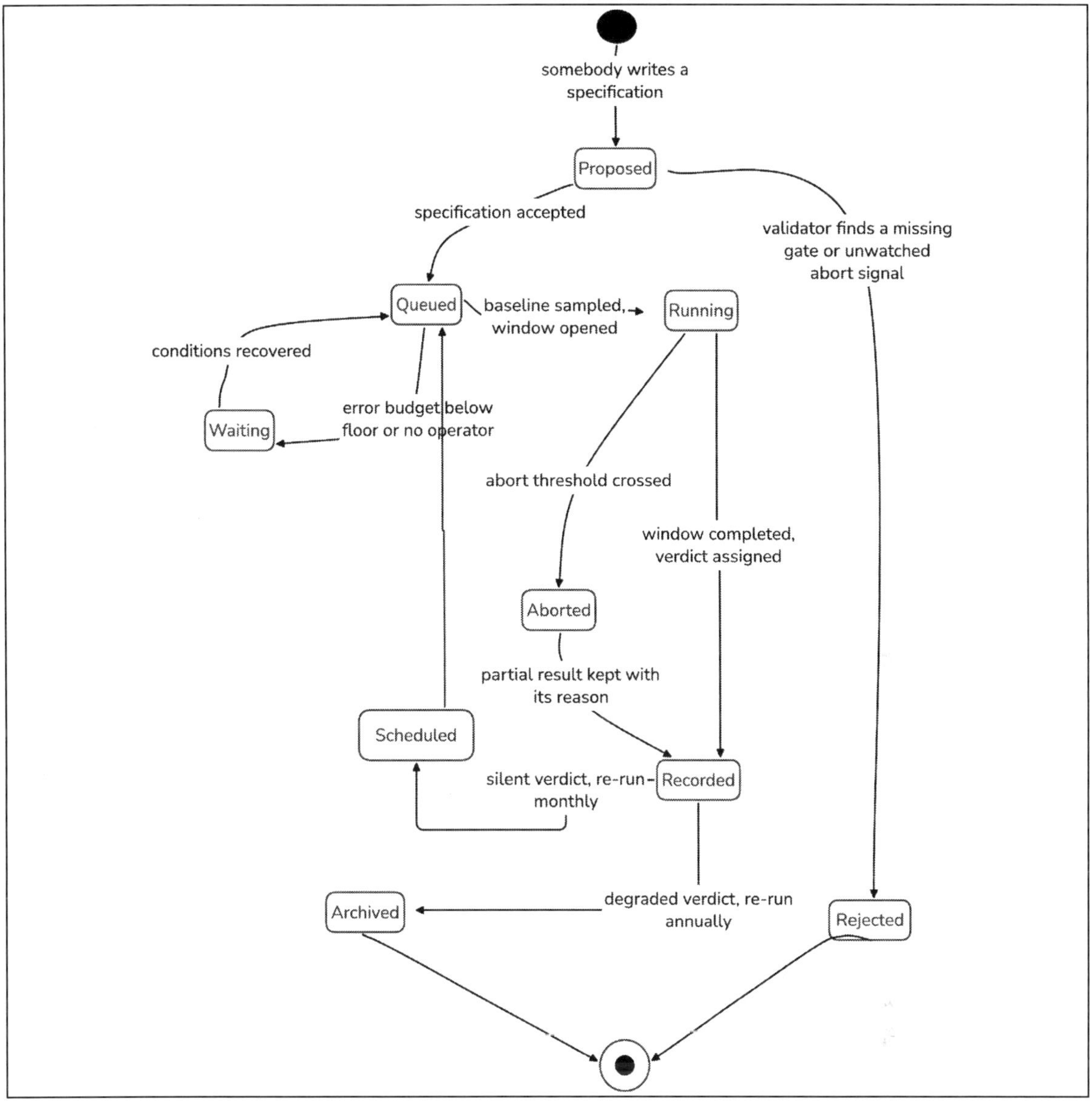

Multi-Tenant Platform Design

A platform capability rather than a team habit needs three properties, and the CNCF end user case study from Flipkart demonstrates all three in production. The tenant isolation keeps one team's experiment inside its own namespace. A central deployment keeps operational cost bounded rather than growing linearly with teams. The parallel injection keeps the platform from becoming the bottleneck it is meant to test.

The first two properties fall out of the Kubernetes primitives our lab already uses. A namespace scoped installation, which is the only supported Litmus mode since the 3.9.0 release, gives isolation for free. A central operation with per team subscription gives cost control. The parallel injection is the one that needs engineering, and Flipkart solved it by replacing on demand helper pods with a node level daemon running concurrent injections.

Game Days and Human Part

Roles and Signal Collision Problem

A continuous schedule does not remove the need for game days, and it changes what they are for. An automated experiment verifies that a known failure mode still produces a known signal. A game day verifies that people can respond, which no schedule can automate. Our roll-up says nothing whatsoever about whether anybody would have known what to do.

A useful exercise needs four roles. Somebody runs the injection and owns the kill switch. Somebody plays incident commander with no special knowledge of what was injected. Somebody observes and records what the responders actually looked at, which is usually more instructive than what they concluded. Finally somebody watches production for real trouble, because the exercise must never become the reason a genuine incident went unnoticed. That last role addresses the signal collision problem, and it deserves a rehearsed answer rather than an improvised one. The responders during an exercise will see abnormal behaviour and must decide whether it belongs to the experiment. Our rule is blunt and has never let us down, since any ambiguity ends the exercise immediately. A hit on the kill switch costs an afternoon of preparation, and guessing wrong costs an outage nobody was watching.

Security-Flavoured Chaos

A certificate expiry, a credential revocation, and a telemetry blackout all make legitimate experiments, and all three carry risks the rest of this book does not. A revoked credential during an exercise can lock out the responders trying to fix it. A disabled telemetry pipeline removes the evidence a real incident would need. A simulated intrusion can trigger genuine escalation paths involving people who did not consent to the exercise.

The difference comes from three precautions. Every security flavoured experiment gets explicit sign off from whoever owns the response process, not merely from engineering. Every one runs with a restore path proven in advance, exactly as the accelerator script in Chapter 4 installed its trap before applying the throttle. Finally, none of them run unattended, since the failure modes here involve people rather than systems.

Summary

We read back forty one recorded experiments and found that 48.8 percent produced no signal the system itself would raise, comfortably above the third predicted in Chapter 1. The rarest verdict proved to be degraded at 9.8 percent, meaning containment with notification is the least common outcome a reliability programme achieves. A fault injected at the accelerator layer surfaced at four different layers, which puts evidence behind the argument that opened this book.

Our signal audit produced the number worth carrying away. Only four of twenty silent results could have been caught by the eight signals derived in Chapter 2, while sixteen needed a signal that did not exist until an experiment demanded it. A signal file is a record of what a practice has learned rather than a specification written in advance. The three gates now run in one command and correctly block the model release that shipped unnoticed six chapters ago, which is where a book about breaking things ought to end.

Index

A

B

C

D

E

F

S

T

U

V

W

Epilogue

It's pretty easy to see where this practice is going next, because the pressure pushing it is arithmetic rather than fashion.

There are three forces all happening at once. One, is autonomous systems that take actions against production infrastructure at a rate no human review process can absorb. There is model behaviour that changes underneath applications without any release taking place, whether through a provider upgrade nobody announced or a retrieval index nobody refreshed. And the last one is, the components carrying these workloads, inference engines, vector stores, agent frameworks, and accelerator schedulers, are younger than the reliability practices being applied to them by roughly a decade. Each force would be manageable on its own. But, together, they're producing a failure profile that our industry hasn't had to deal with before. Basically, systems are degrading continuously, silently, and without any single event to investigate afterwards.

I'm expecting three developments over the next few years. Quality signals will become first-class operational telemetry rather than something the data science team owns, because the alternative is running blind. Autonomous actions will get gated the way deployments got gated, once enough organisations have traced a cascade back to a well-intentioned remediation agent. At the end of the day, the golden set is going to be as standard as the health check, since comparing against recorded truth is the only way to spot any of this. There's no need for any new research. All the techniques in this book are based on published prior art, standard statistics and tools that are available today under permissive licences. What's needed is someone to decide that the work is worth an afternoon. The consequences of not doing it need to be made clear, because it won't be an outage.

If a team skips this work, they won't have a big failure to learn from. They get a system that's quietly serving worse results month after month, and the staff are working a bit harder to make up for it, until someone outside the organisation notices. Support agents tend to override more drafts. The customers escalate more often. Some people think it's down to the time of year, a tough quarter, or the model provider having a bad week. By the time anyone measures it properly, the degradation has been building up for so long that no one can say when it started. And such outcome is worse than an outage in one specific way. When there's an outage, you end up with a timeline, a root cause and a fix. Silent degradation doesn't produce any of those, so you can't learn from it and it tends to happen again. The same thing was said by organisations that had experienced it. They said they couldn't tell if the system was working or not.

The good news is that the solution is out there and ready to use. It's a good idea to write down what the right behaviour looks like. And break things on purpose, on a schedule, inside a window where someone's watching. You need to record what happened in a way that you can query it in six months. Think about how often you've been left in the dark.

After that, just reduce that number.

--Neel Trove

Thank You

Made in United States
Orlando, FL
04 November 2026

90200386R00114